SEMAPRO 2018

The Twelfth International Conference on Advances in Semantic Processing

November 18 - 22, 2018

Athens, Greece

SEMAPRO 2018 Editors

Michael Spranger, Hochschule Mittweida, University of Applied Sciences, Germany

Pascal Lorenz, University of Haute Alsace, France

Printed from e-media with permission by:

Curran Associates, Inc.
57 Morehouse Lane
Red Hook, NY 12571

Some format issues inherent in the e-media version may also appear in this print version.

Printed by Curran Associates, Inc. (2019)

International Academy, Research, and Industry Association (IARIA)
412 Derby Way
Wilmington, DE 19810

Phone: (408) 893-6407
Fax: (408) 527-6351

petre@iaria.org

Additional copies of this publication are available from:

Curran Associates, Inc.
57 Morehouse Lane
Red Hook, NY 12571 USA
Phone: 845-758-0400
Fax: 845-758-2633
Email: curran@proceedings.com
Web: www.proceedings.com

Table of Contents

Investigating Argument Relatedness Based on Linguistic Knowledge 1
Marie Garnier, Sarah Bourse, and Patrick Saint-Dizier

Word Embeddings of Monosemous Words in Dictionary for Word Sense Disambiguation 4
Minoru Sasaki

An Ontology for Cultural Heritage Protection against Climate Change 8
Jurgen Mossgraber, Paraskevi Pouli, Desiree Hilbring, Guiseppina Padeletti, and Tobias Hellmund

A Survey of Ontology Learning from Text 14
Kaoutar Belhoucine and Mohammed Mourchid

Towards an Automated System for Music Event Detection 22
Jian Xi, Michael Spranger, Hanna Siewerts, and Dirk Labudde

Italian Domain-specific Thesaurus as a Means of Semantic Control for Cybersecurity Terminology 28
Claudia Lanza

Extended Functionality of Mathematical Formulae Search Service 35
Alexander Gusenkov, Polina Gusenkova, Yana Palacheva, and Olga Zhibrik

Tedi: a Platform for Ontologisation of Multilingual Terminologies for the Semantic Web 42
Maria Papadopoulou and Christophe Roche

Estimating Semantic Similarity for Targeted Marketing based on Fuzzy Sets and the Odenet Ontology 48
Tim vor der Bruck

SEMAPRO 2018

Forward

The Twelfth International Conference on Advances in Semantic Processing (SEMAPRO 2018), held between November 18, 2018 and November 22, 2018 in Athens, Greece, continued a series of events that were initiated considering the complexity of understanding and processing information. Semantic processing considers contextual dependencies and adds to the individually acquired knowledge emergent properties and understanding. Hardware and software support and platforms were developed for semantically enhanced information retrieval and interpretation. Searching for video, voice and speech [VVS] raises additional problems to specialized engines with respect to text search. Contextual searching and special patterns-based techniques are current solutions.

With the progress on ontology, web services, semantic social media, semantic web, deep web search /deep semantic web/, semantic deep web, semantic networking and semantic reasoning, SEMAPRO 2018 constituted the stage for the state-of-the-art on the most recent advances.

The conference had the following tracks:

- Basics on semantics
- Domain-oriented semantic applications
- Semantic applications/platforms/tools

We take here the opportunity to warmly thank all the members of the SEMAPRO 2018 technical program committee, as well as all the reviewers. The creation of such a high quality conference program would not have been possible without their involvement. We also kindly thank all the authors that dedicated much of their time and effort to contribute to SEMAPRO 2018. We truly believe that, thanks to all these efforts, the final conference program consisted of top quality contributions.

We also gratefully thank the members of the SEMAPRO 2018 organizing committee for their help in handling the logistics and for their work that made this professional meeting a success.

We hope that SEMAPRO 2018 was a successful international forum for the exchange of ideas and results between academia and industry and to promote further progress in the field of semantic processing. We also hope that Athens, Greece, provided a pleasant environment during the conference and everyone saved some time to enjoy the historic charm of the city.

SEMAPRO 2018 Chairs

SEMAPRO Steering Committee

Fabio Grandi, University of Bologna, Italy
Tassilo Pellegrini, St. Pölten University of Applied Sciences, Austria

Sandra Lovrenčić, University of Zagreb, Croatia
Giuseppe Berio, Université de Bretagne Sud / IRISA, France
Takahiro Kawamura, Japan Science and Technology Agency (JST), Japan
Sule Yildirim Yayilgan, Gjøvik University College, Norway
Michele Melchiori, Università degli Studi di Brescia, Italy
Muhammad Javed, Cornell University, USA
Wladyslaw Homenda, Warsaw University of Technology, Poland

SEMAPRO Industry/Research Advisory Committee

Enrico Francesconi, ITTIG-CNR / Publications Office of the EU, Italy
Peera Pacharintanakul, TOT, Thailand
Mari Wigham, Wageningen Food & Biobased Research, The Netherlands
Raoul G. C. Schönhof, High Performance Computing Center Stuttgart (HLRS), Germany
Raghava Mutharaju, GE Global Research, Niskayuna, USA
Riccardo Albertoni, Istituto per la Matematica Applicata e Tecnologie Informatiche "Enrico Magenes" - Consiglio Nazionale delle Ricerche (IMATI-CNR), Italy
Sofia Athenikos, Bank of America Merrill Lynch, USA
Shun Hattori, Muroran Institute of Technology, Japan

SEMAPRO 2018
Committee

SEMAPRO Steering Committee

Fabio Grandi, University of Bologna, Italy
Tassilo Pellegrini, St. Pölten University of Applied Sciences, Austria
Sandra Lovrenčić, University of Zagreb, Croatia
Giuseppe Berio, Université de Bretagne Sud / IRISA, France
Takahiro Kawamura, Japan Science and Technology Agency (JST), Japan
Sule Yildirim Yayilgan, Gjøvik University College, Norway
Michele Melchiori, Università degli Studi di Brescia, Italy
Muhammad Javed, Cornell University, USA
Wladyslaw Homenda, Warsaw University of Technology, Poland

SEMAPRO Industry/Research Advisory Committee

Enrico Francesconi, ITTIG-CNR / Publications Office of the EU, Italy
Peera Pacharintanakul, TOT, Thailand
Mari Wigham, Wageningen Food & Biobased Research, The Netherlands
Raoul G. C. Schönhof, High Performance Computing Center Stuttgart (HLRS), Germany
Raghava Mutharaju, GE Global Research, Niskayuna, USA
Riccardo Albertoni, Istituto per la Matematica Applicata e Tecnologie Informatiche "Enrico Magenes" - Consiglio Nazionale delle Ricerche (IMATI-CNR), Italy
Sofia Athenikos, Bank of America Merrill Lynch, USA
Shun Hattori, Muroran Institute of Technology, Japan

SEMAPRO 2018 Technical Program Committee

Riccardo Albertoni, Istituto per la Matematica Applicata e Tecnologie Informatiche "Enrico Magenes" -Consiglio Nazionale delle Ricerche (IMATI-CNR), Italy
Jose María Alvarez Rodríguez, Carlos III University of Madrid, Spain
Marta Andersson, Stockholm University, Sweden
Sofia Athenikos, Bank of America Merrill Lynch, USA
Agnese Augello, ICAR - Istituto di Calcolo e Reti ad alte prestazioni | Consiglio Nazionale delle Ricerche, Palermo, Italy
Isabel Azevedo, Instituto Superior de Engenharia do Porto (ISEP), Porto, Portugal
Samira Babalou, Friedrich Schiller University of Jena, Germany
Carlos Badenes-Olmedo, Universidad Politécnica de Madrid (UPM), Spain
Fernanda Baiao, Federal University of the State of Rio de Janeiro, Brazil
Jarosław Bąk, Poznan University of Technology, Poland
Phạm The Bao, University of Science - Ho Chi Minh City, Vietnam
Giuseppe Berio, Université de Bretagne Sud / IRISA, France

Jorge Bernardino, Polytechnic of Coimbra - ISEC, Portugal
Stefano Bortoli, HUAWEI TECHNOLOGIES Duesseldorf GmbH - German Research Center - Munich Office, Germany
Loris Bozzato, Fondazione Bruno Kessler, Trento, Italy
Zouhaier Brahmia, University of Sfax, Tunisia
Okan Bursa, Ege University, Turkey
Özgü Can, Ege University, Turkey
Rodrigo Capobianco Guido, São Paulo State University (UNESP), Brazil
Elena Cardillo, Institute of Informatics and Telematics - National Research Council, Italy
Julio Cesar Duarte, Military Institute of Engineering (IME), Brazil
Mingmin Chen, Uber Inc., USA
Muhao Chen, University of California Los Angeles, USA
Christos Christodoulopoulos, Amazon Research Cambridge, UK
Ioannis Chrysakis, Foundation for Research and Technology-Hellas, Institute of Computer Science (FORTH-ICS), Greece
Francesco Corcoglioniti, Fondazione Bruno Kessler - Trento, Italy
Valentin Cristea, University Politehnica Bucharest, Romania
Ademar Crotti Junior, Trinity College Dublin, Ireland
Zhihua Cui, Taiyuan University of Science and Technology, China
Mariana Damova, Mozajka Ltd, Bulgaria
Cláudio de Souza Baptista, Federal University of Campina Grande, Brazil
Maria Teresa Chiaravalloti, Institute of Informatics and Telematics | National Research Council of Italy, Italy
Amitava Das, Indian Institute of Information Technology, Andhra Pradesh, India
Monica De Martino, IMATI - National Research Council, Italy
Anastasia Dimou, Ghent University - IDLab – imec, Belgium
Melike Sah Direkoglu, Near East University, North Cyprus
Christian Dirschl, Wolters Kluwer Deutschland GmbH, Germany
Milan Dojchinovski, InfAI, Leipzig University, Germany / Czech Technical University in Prague, Czech Republic
Mauro Dragoni, Fondazione Bruno Kessler (FBK-IRST), Italy
Surya Durbha, Indian Institute of Technology Bombay (IITB), India
Ivan Ermilov, University of Leipzig, Germany
Vadim Ermolayev, Zaporozhye National University, Ukraine
Diego Esteves, University of Bonn, Germany
Muhammad Fahad, Centre Scientifique et Technique du Batiment CSTB (Sophia-Antipolis), France
Enrico Francesconi, ITTIG-CNR / Publications Office of the EU, Italy
Panorea Gaitanou, Ionian University, Greece
Marcos Garcia, University of Coruña, Galiza, Spain
Chetana Gavankar, Cummins College of Engineering for Women, India
José M. Giménez-García, Université Jean Monnet, Saint-Étienne, France
Tatjana Gornostaja, Tilde, Latvia
Natalia Grabar, Université Lille 3, France

Fabio Grandi, University of Bologna, Italy
William Grosky, University of Michigan, USA
Ali Hasnain, National University of Ireland Galway, Ireland
Shun Hattori, Muroran Institute of Technology, Japan
Abdelati Hawwari, The George Washington University, USA
Benjamin Heitmann, Fraunhofer Institute for Applied Information Technology FIT, Germany
Gerald Hiebel, University of Innsbruck, Austria
Armin Hoenen, Johann Wolfgang Goethe-Universität Frankfurt am Main, Germany
Tracy Holloway King, Amazon, USA
Wladyslaw Homenda, Warsaw University of Technology, Poland
Tzung-Pei Hong, National University of Kaohsiung, Taiwan
Thomas Hubauer, Siemens AG Corporate Technology, Germany
Sergio Ilarri, University of Zaragoza, Spain
Ludger Jansen, Institut für Philosophie | Universität Rostock, Germany
Agnieszka Jastrzębska, Warsaw University of Technology, Poland
Muhammad Javed, Cornell University, USA
Takahiro Kawamura, Japan Science and Technology Agency (JST), Japan
Haklae Kim, KISTI (Korea Institute of Science and Technology Information), Korea
Young-Gab Kim, Sejong University, Seoul, Korea
Gerda Koch, AIT Angewandte Informationstechnik Forschungsgesellschaft mbH, Austria
Mieczyslaw "Mitch" M. Kokar, Northeastern University, Boston, USA
Stasinos Konstantopoulos, Institute of Informatics and Telecommunications, NCSR "Demokritos", Greece
Efstratios Kontopoulos, Information Technologies Institute (ITI) / Center for Research & Technology Hellas (CERTH), Greece
Petr Kremen, Czech Technical University in Prague, Czech Republic
Jaroslav Kuchař, Czech Technical University in Prague, Czech Republic
Kyu-Chul Lee, Chungnam National University, Republic of Korea
Els Lefever, Ghent University, Belgium
Antonio Lieto, University of Turin and ICAR-CNR, Italy
Yunfei Long, Hong Kong Polytechnic University, Hong Kong
Giuseppe Loseto, Polytechnic University of Bari, Italy
Sandra Lovrenčić, University of Zagreb, Croatia
Wencan Luo, University of Pittsburgh, USA
Federica Mandreoli, Universita' di Modena e Reggio Emilia, Italy
Miguel Felix Mata Rivera, UPIITA-IPN, Mexico
Brigitte Mathiak, GESIS - Leibniz institute for Social Sciences, Germany
John McCrae, Insight Centre for Data Analytics | National University of Ireland, Galway, Ireland
Imen Megdiche, Institut National Universitaire Champollion | IRIT, France
Michele Melchiori, Università degli Studi di Brescia, Italy
Panagiotis Mitzias, Information Technologies Institute (ITI) of the Centre for Research & Technology Hellas (CERTH), Greece
Najmeh Mousavi Nejad, University of Bonn / Fraunhofer IAIS, Germany
Diego Moussallem, University of Leipzig, Germany

Raghava Mutharaju, GE Global Research, Niskayuna, USA
Yotaro Nakayama, Technology Research & Innovation, Nihon Unisys Ltd., Tokyo Japan
Sangha Nam, KAIST, South Korea
Fatemeh Nargesian, University of Toronto, Canada
Nikolay Nikolov, SINTEF Digital, Norway
Lyndon Nixon, MODUL Technology GmbH, Austria
Fabrizio Orlandi, University of Bonn and Fraunhofer IAIS, Germany
Peera Pacharintanakul, TOT, Thailand
Peteris Paikens, University of Latvia, Latvia
Panagiotis Papadakos, FORTH-ICS (Foundation for Research and Technology - Hellas, Institute of Computer Science), Greece
Tassilo Pellegrini, St. Pölten University of Applied Sciences, Austria
Rivindu Perera, Auckland University of Technology, New Zealand
Vassilios Peristeras, International Hellenic University, Greece
Silvia Piccini, Istituto di Linguistica Computazionale «A. Zampolli» - CNR, Italy
Octavian Popescu, IBM T. J. Watson Research Center, USA
Livia Predoiu, University of Oxford, UK
Behrang Qasemizadeh, Heinrich-Heine-Universität Düsseldorf, Germany
Livy Real, University of Sao Paulo, Brazil
Georg Rehm, DFKI GmbH, Germany
Irene Renau, Pontificia Universidad Católica de Valparaíso, Chile
Kate Revoredo, Federal University of the State of Rio de Janeiro - UNIRIO, Brazil
German Rigau Claramunt, University of the Basque Country, Spain
Juergen Rilling, Concordia University, Montreal, Canada
Tarmo Robal, Tallinn University of Technology, Estonia
Alejandro Rodríguez González, Universidad Politécnica de Madrid, Spain
Jacqueline Rosette, Swansea University, UK
Michele Ruta, Technical University of Bari, Italy
Patrick Saint-Dizier, IRIT, France
Minoru Sasaki, Ibaraki University, Japan
Stefan Schlobach, Vrije Universiteit Amsterdam, Netherlands
Raoul G. C. Schönhof, High Performance Computing Center Stuttgart (HLRS), Germany
Kinga Schumacher, German Research Center for Artificial Intelligence (DFKI GmbH), Germany
Anne-Kathrin Schumann, ProTechnology GmbH, Dresden, Germany
Wieland Schwinger, Johannes Kepler University Linz (JKU) | Inst. f. Telekooperation (TK), Linz, Austria
Floriano Scioscia, Polytechnic University of Bari, Italy
Emine Sezer, Ege Universitesi, Izmir, Turkey
Nuno Silva, School of Engineering - Polytechnic of Porto, Portugal
Vasco N. G. J. Soares, Instituto de Telecomunicações / Instituto Politécnico de Castelo Branco, Portugal
Ahmet Soylu, Norwegian University of Science and Technology / SINTEF Digital, Norway
Lars G. Svensson, Deutsche Nationalbibliothek, Germany

George Tambouratzis, Institute for Language and Speech Processing, Athena, Greece
WeldeRufael B. Tesfay, Deutsche Telekom Chair of Mobile Business and Multilateral Security | Goethe University Frankfurt, Germany
Christos Tryfonopoulos, University of the Peloponnese, Greece
Jouni Tuominen, University of Helsinki, Finland
Murat Osman Ünalir, Ege University, Turkey
Jung-Ho Um, KISTI (Korea Institute of Science and Technology Information), Republic of Korea
Taketoshi Ushiama, Kyushu University, Japan
Jack Verhoosel, Netherlands Organisation for Applied Scientific Research (TNO), Netherlands
Sirje Virkus, Tallinn University, Estonia
Daiva Vitkute-Adzgauskiene, Vytautas Magnus University, Lithuania
Tim vor der Brück, Lucerne University of Applied Sciences and Arts, Switzerland
Rita Zaharah Wan-Chik, Malaysian Institute of Information Technology (MIIT) - Universiti Kuala Lumpur, Malaysia
Yingying Wang, Snap Research, USA
Mari Wigham, Wageningen Food & Biobased Research, The Netherlands
Wai Lok Woo, Newcastle University, UK
Adam Zachary Wyner, Swansea University, UK
Sule Yildirim Yayilgan, Gjøvik University College, Norway
Alexander Yohan, University of Science and Technology, Taiwan
Roberto Yus, University of California, Irvine, USA
Fouad Zablith, Olayan School of Business | American University of Beirut, Lebanon
Stefan Zander, Hochschule Darmstadt, Germany
Martin Zelm, INTEROP-VLab, Brussels, Belgium
Xiaowang Zhang, Tianjin University, China
Ziqi Zhang, Nottingham Trent University, UK
Lihua Zhao, National Institute of Advanced Industrial Science and Technology (AIST), Tokyo, Japan

Copyright Information

Investigating Argument Relatedness Based on Linguistic Knowledge

Marie Garnier, Sarah Bourse

Cultures Anglo-Saxonnes
Université Toulouse 2 Jean Jaurès
5 allée Antonio Machado
31058 Toulouse, France
Email: mgarnier@univ-tlse2.fr,
sarah.bourse@univ-tlse2.fr

Patrick Saint-Dizier

CNRS - IRIT
118 route de Narbonne
31062 Toulouse Cedex France
Email: stdizier@irit.fr

***Abstract*—In this contribution, we explore the type of linguistic knowledge that is required to establish relatedness between a claim and a justification which may be distant or in different texts, within the framework of argument mining. We propose an original annotation method based on XML-Frames and a linguistic analysis of the main resources which are needed to establish relatedness on a linguistic basis.**

***Keywords*–Argument Mining; Linguistic Knowledge; Relatedness; Annotation.**

I. Aims and Motivations

One of the main challenges of argument mining is to correctly identify the statements that are justifications or that support a given claim across different types of online texts (for example, news articles, blogs, consumer reviews). This issue is called argument relatedness and it is a central point in information retrieval. It is also essential in argument mining [1]-[3]. The main objective of research on argument relatedness is to be able to mine statements which develop the same topic as the given claim and have an argumentative orientation. Broadly speaking, relatedness is a measure of the semantic and topical proximity of two text spans. These segments may differ lexically (via the use of synonyms, hyponyms or hypernyms, to name a few possibilities) or syntactically (for example, with alternations, such as active vs. passive structures). Previous research [4] has shown that establishing relatedness between an argument and a statement requires knowledge in 58% to 88% of situations, depending on the topic of the claim.

Since supports and attacks (elements that oppose a claim) of a claim mainly address the purposes, goals, functions or structure of the main concepts of the claim, previous studies have used the Qualia structure of the Generative Lexicon [5] as a knowledge representation system for relatedness. This approach pairs domain knowledge with lexical semantics in an efficient and principled way. However, this previous work also shows that Qualia structures are difficult to develop and must be defined for each topic. This makes knowledge-based argument mining an approach that, although effective, is difficult to reuse over different domains.

The current research project examines and evaluates the possibility of establishing relatedness solely on the basis of linguistic knowledge and lexical semantics. The development of general-purpose linguistic processes and resources that characterize relatedness would make the implementation of relatedness much simpler and much more reusable over domains. This contribution explores this hypothesis as well as the linguistic knowledge which is required, in particular lexical semantics.

The rest of the paper is structured as follows. The analysis protocol and the annotation system are presented in Section II, while Section III deals with the future steps that need to be taken to be able to establish relatedness on a linguistic basis.

II. Analysis Protocol

This research introduces two specificities. First, the analysis of relatedness is based on the topical content of the claim, as a claim-driven analysis allows the analysis to focus on the features of the claim and to integrate the new elements found in various statements related to that claim. In addition, the annotation is not based on standard linear text annotations but on the use of frames encoded in XML: the use of an XML-Frame approach is motivated by the fact that the elements found in statements and that are decisive for the analysis of the semantic elements of relatedness may not be adjacent, which makes text annotation, which is linear, almost intractable.

In this framework, relevant statements are extracted from the source text and fed into XML-Frames in which the features are filled in manually by annotators. Each statement found to be related to the claim and with an argumentative orientation originates an instance of the frame. The result is a set of frames which can be organized as a tree, where the root is the frame representing the claim and the children are those statements found in texts and that introduce additional constraints on the topic. These additional constraints on the claim topic characterize relatedness.

The relations of each statement with the claim are described in each frame instance through the use of features indicating the linguistic and conceptual links between the claim and the statement. Our corpus is based on texts about controversial social issues, addressing topics such as affirmative action or the gender pay gap. These are relatively complex issues, which guarantees that the need for linguistic and conceptual knowledge will be apparent. The goal is then to mine statements which are related to this claim in various texts. These statements must have a topic that is subsumed by the claim topic and an argumentative orientation which may support or attack the claim, depending on the content of the statement. The argumentative orientation is given by evaluative expressions such as scalar adjectives, possibly modified by an adverb of intensity. Those statements are also frequently associated with discourse structures which further develop them.

The frame template we have defined for the study of relatedness is very detailed. Inside the general frame <statement>, four sub-frames are embedded (<topic>, <evaluative>, <discourse>, <arg_scheme>), with the first two subframes also including two additional subframes which allow for the identification of a main topic and a field of application for this topic.

As an illustration, let us consider the following claim: *affirmative action in education is good for the economy*. This claim is composed of a topic: *affirmative action in education* and an evaluative expression: *is good for the economy*. The topic is itself composed of a main concept, *affirmative action* and a field of application for this concept, *in education*. The evaluative expression is analyzed in the same way (*is good* and *for the economy*). The annotation scheme is presented below in more detail:

```
<statement> <topic> <top_main markers= ,
   link= , concept_op= ,
   restrictions= ,
   annotator_confidence= >,
   <top_field markers= , link= ,
   concept_op= ,
   restrictions= ,
   annotator_confidence= >   <\topic>
<evaluative> <ev_main markers= ,
   polarity= , strength= ,
   restrictions= ,
   annotator_confidence= >,
   <ev_field markers= , link= ,
   concept_op= ,
   restrictions= ,
   annotator_confidence= >
 <\evaluative>
<discourse> <text= , type= > </discourse>
<arg_scheme
    type= , annotator_confidence= >
<\statement>
```

To say it briefly, this frame allows the description of most features that characterize relatedness. The 'link' and 'concept_op' features respectively specify the linguistic link (exact words, derivation, semantic field, etc.) and the conceptual operation taking place between the words of the claim and the words of the text (reformulation, summarization, definition, etc.). The same description is made for the evaluative expression with, in addition, the orientation and strength of the evaluation.

The <discourse> subframe describes elements such as elaborations, illustrations, comparisons, conditions or circumstances that are not directly argumentative but can be seen as being part of the argument. Finally, the annotator is invited to specify the kind of argument scheme(s) that has been used, from a standard list of arguments [6] [7].

III. Toward a Linguistic Categorization of Relatedness

The 'link' and 'concept_op' features are specifically designed to allow for the linguistic categorization of relatedness. To describe the linguistic and conceptual links with the claim, the annotators can use predefined categories or natural language, until a stable list of categories can emerge through the collective observation and analysis of the corpus. Then, a categorization of the main linguistic operations can be carried out, and the associated resources can be developed and structured from existing resources. The aim of this categorization is to characterize the linguistic operations behind relatedness and to evaluate the efficiency and scope of a linguistic approach, i.e. how much of relatedness analysis can be resolved via linguistic processes.

The parameters which are under investigation, categorization and evaluation are as follows:

- the paradigmatic lexico-semantic transformations developed from the topic of the claim and its restrictions, in particular, forms of synonymy, partial reformulations (*the lower representation of women in paid work*), paraphrases, restrictions, opposites, forms of inchoativity (terms describing the result instead of the process) or vice-versa (for example: *gender pay parity* $\rightarrow$ *gender pay gap*).

- the functional transformations which are related to the nature of the topic, and may induce some domain dependent lexical data (for example: *providing a better balance of job opportunities for all)*. These functional terms are derived from linguistic resources that develop the goals or purposes of entities. These may be found, for the simplest kinds, in WordNet (examples and data can be found in [13]).

- the local syntactic transformations on the claim topic, (*the gap in salary between genders)*,

- forms of discourse transformations such as: summarization (when the topic is long), illustration or instantiation, expression of consequence,

- the lexical data which is necessary, its structure according to lexical semantics principles [8], and its availability. A number of resources are already present in our <TextCoop> platform that realizes discourse analysis in English and French with high accuracy (about 90% accuracy in the case of the domains considered here). The version 5.1 of this platform is available at [14] while system foundations and examples can be found in [15].

Acknowledgments

This research project is partly funded by a grant from the Maison des Sciences de l'Humain et de la Société, Université de Toulouse, France.

References

[1] R. Mochales Palau and M.F. Moens, "Argumentation mining: the detection, classification and structure of arguments in text." In Proceedings of the 12th International Conference on Artificial Intelligence and Law, pp. 98-107, 2009.

[2] A. Peldszus and M. Stede, "From argument diagrams to argumentation mining in texts: a survey." In International Journal of Cognitive Informatics and Natural Intelligence (IJCINI), vol. 7, no 1, pp. 1-31, 2013.

[3] R. Swanson, B. Ecker and M. Walker, "Argument mining: extracting arguments from online dialogue," In Proceedings of the 16th Annual Meeting of the Special Interest Group on Discourse and Dialogue, pp. 217-226, 2015.

[4] P. Saint-Dizier, "Argument Mining: the bottleneck of knowledge and lexical resources," In Proceedings of the 10th International Conference on Language Resources and Evaluation (LREC 2016), pp. 977-983, 2016.

[5] J. Pustejovsky, The Generative Lexicon, MIT Press, 1995.

[6] D. Walton, C. Reed, and F. Macagno, Argumentation Schemes, Cambridge University Press, 2008.

[7] V. W. Feng and G. Hirst, "Classifying arguments by scheme." In Proceedings of the 49th Annual Meeting of the Association for Computational Linguistics: Human Language Technologies, vol. 1, pp. 987-996, 2011.

[8] A. Cruse, Lexical Semantics, Cambridge University Press, 1986.

[9] A. Fiedler and H. Horacek, "Argumentation within deductive reasoning." International Journal of Intelligent Systems, 22(1):49-70, 2007.

[10] H. Nguyen and D. Litman, "Extracting argument and domain words for identifying argument components in texts." In Proceedings of the 2nd Workshop on Argumentation Mining, pp. 22-28, 2015.

[11] M. P. Villalba and P. Saint-Dizier, "Some facets of argument mining for opinion analysis," COMMA, vol. 245, pp. 23-34, 2012.

[12] M. Walker, P. Anand, J.E. Fox Tree, R. Abbott and J. King, "A corpus for research on deliberation and debate," In LREC, pp. 812-817, 2012.

[13] WordNet presentation and database access, last version available at: https://wordnet.princeton.edu/, Princeton University, 2018.

[14] TextCoop archive, V5.1, freeware, available at: https://www.irit.fr/'tilde'Patrick.Saint-Dizier/#projets., CNRS, IRIT, Toulouse, 2012.

[15] P. Saint-Dizier, Challenges of Discourse Processing: the case of technical documents, Cambridge Scholars Publishing, 2014.

Word Embeddings of Monosemous Words in Dictionary for Word Sense Disambiguation

Minoru Sasaki
Dept. of Computer and Information Sciences
Faculty of Engineering, Ibaraki University
4-12-1, Nakanarusawa, Hitachi, Ibaraki, 316-8511, Japan
Email: minoru.sasaki.01@vc.ibaraki.ac.jp

Abstract—**In the recent past, word embedding techniques have shown to capture semantic and syntactic information of natural language which could be exploited to solve the Word Sense Disambiguation (WSD) task. Word embeddings are generated using words appearing in context. However, some co-occurrence words in context have multiple meanings and are ambiguous. Therefore, it is sometimes difficult to identify the meaning of a target word by using word embeddings of context words. In this paper, we propose to use word embeddings of monosemous words for the WSD task. We consider that word embeddings of monosemous words can contribute to determining the correct sense of a target word. Also, by using word dependency in a sentence, it is possible to capture the semantic relationship between the target word and the co-occurrence word as a feature. To evaluate the efficiency of the proposed WSD method, we show that it is effective for the WSD task to use both monosemous word information and dependency relation to the target word.**

Keywords-word sense disambiguation; monosemous words; word embeddings.

I. Introduction

Typically, many words have multiple meanings, depending on the context in which they are used. Identifying the sense of a polysemous word within a given context is a fundamental problem in natural language processing. For example, an English word "bank" have different senses, such as "a commercial bank" or "a land along the edge of a river" etc. Word Sense Disambiguation (WSD) is the task of deciding the appropriate meaning of a target ambiguous word in its context [9].

To solve the computational WSD problem, it is usually formulated as a classification task, where the possible word senses are the classes. In the supervised learning method, bag-of-words features extracted from a wide context window around the target word are used. In the recent past, word embedding techniques (e.g., word2vec) have shown to capture semantic and syntactic information of natural language and improve performance of the WSD task [7].

In word2vec, word embeddings are generated using words appearing in context. However, some co-occurrence words in context have multiple meanings and are ambiguous. Therefore, it is sometimes difficult to identify the meaning of a target word by using word embeddings of context words. For example, if the polysemous word "flow" appears in the context, it is not possible to distinguish the meaning of the target word "bank". However, if the monosemous word "financial" appears in the context, it is easy to distinguish the meaning of the "bank". For the word "flow", word2vec creates a word embedding containing these multiple meanings. So, these features are not effective to distinguish a target word due to its association with polysemous words. Therefore, we would like to focus on solving this issue and explore the effective features for training WSD classifiers.

In this paper, we propose a new method for WSD using word embeddings of the monosemous words in context and word dependency. We consider that word embeddings of monosemous words can contribute to determining the correct sense of a target word. Also, by using word dependency in a sentence, it is possible to capture the semantic relationship between the target word and the co-occurrence word as a feature. We show that word embeddings of monosemous words in dependency relation to the target word is effective for word sense disambiguation.

The rest of this paper is organized as follows. Section I I is devoted to the related work in the literature. Section III describes the proposed WSD methods using word embeddings of the monosemous words. In Section IV, we describe an outline of experiments and experimental results. Finally, Section V concludes the paper.

II. Related Works

Numerous works have recently demonstrated the effectiveness of bag-of-words model on WSD tasks. In supervised WSD, each occurrence of a polysemous word is converted into a small number of local features that include co-occurrence and part-of-speech information near the target word [14]. In this paper, we focus on supervised WSD using word embeddings.

Word embeddings are low-dimensional vector representations of words, based on the distributional contexts in which words appear. Word embeddings are effective at capturing intuitive characteristics of the words and can be generally useful in many NLP tasks [4][11]. Word embeddings as local context features have been used in supervised learning approaches [13].

Monosemous words can be employed to represent word contexts. Li et al. proposed the Chinese WSD method using monosemous words as features [6]. However, this method can only use limited monosemous words obtained from the Chinese thesaurus Cilin and does not use word embeddings based on neural networks. Moreover, the effectiveness of monosemous words was not verified in the Japanese WSD task. Li et al. point out that the WSD system tends to have low precision when the usage of a polysemous word is inconsistent with the monosemous words in the same class.

To obtain precise usage information, syntactic information, such as dependency relations of words has been employed. Some works exploited the dependency relations represented by the linguistic unit called bunsetsu [5][8]. These researches report that the syntactic relations are effective for WSD and document retrieval tasks. In our WSD method, we employ word embeddings of the monosemous words in context and word dependency as features and evaluate the efficiency of this WSD method.

III. WSD Methods

A. Task Description

A WSD system is used to select the appropriate sense for a target polysemous word in context. WSD can be viewed as a classification task in which each target word should be classified into one of the predefined existing senses. Word senses were annotated in a corpus in accordance with "Iwanami's Japanese Dictionary (The Iwanami Kokugo Jiten)". It has three levels for sense IDs and the middle-level sense is used in this task.

In this paper, supervised classification is employed for this WSD task. This supervised method requires a corpus of manually labeled training data to construct classifiers for every polysemous word. Then, each obtained classifier is applied to a set of unlabeled examples.

B. Supervised WSD methods

In this section, we briefly describe the baseline WSD method and our three WSD method using word embeddings of the monosemous words in context and word dependency. The first method is the WSD method using word embeddings of the only monosemous words in context. The second one is the WSD method using word embeddings of the words that have direct dependency relations with the target word. The third one is the WSD method using word embeddings of both the monosemous words and the words that have direct dependency relations with the target word.

In our experiments, we use the supervised learning approach to obtain the WSD models. The training set used to learn the models contains a set of examples in which a given target word is manually tagged with a sense. Each sentence is segmented into words by a morphological analyzer. Part-of-speech tags are assigned to the obtained words that are lemmatized.

1) The Baseline System: The baseline system uses word embeddings of the words in a sentence. In this baseline system, we calculate the average of word embeddings of all words except the target word in a sentence. Then, a supervised WSD classifier for the target word is constructed from a training set of the average vectors of input sentences and their appropriate sense label (Figure 1).

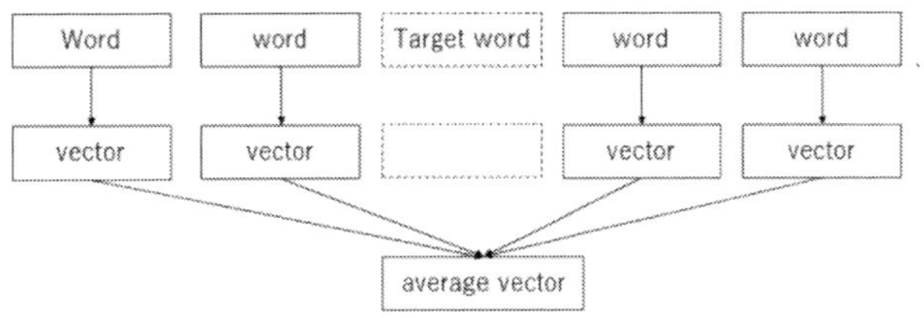

Fig. 1. Baseline System.

2) WSD using word embeddings of the only monosemous words: This WSD system employs word embeddings of the only monosemous words in context. A monosemous word is defined as as a word that has only one meaning in the "Iwanami's Japanese Dictionary (The Iwanami Kokugo Jiten)". In this system, we extract monosemous words in the two words either side of the target word and represent their word embeddings. Then, a WSD classifier for the target word is constructed from a training set of their word embeddings and their appropriate sense label (Figure 2).

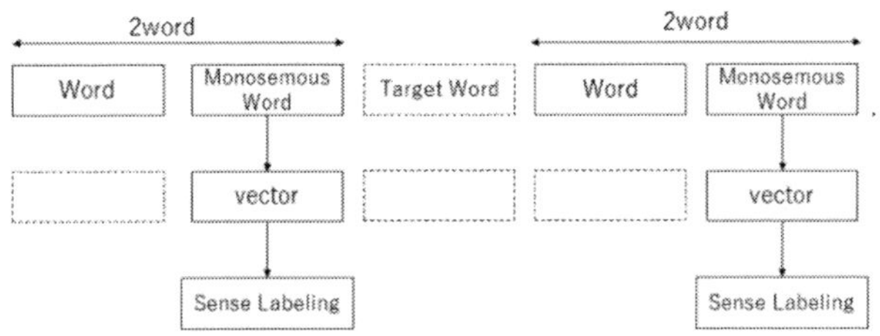

Fig. 2. WSD Using Word Embeddings of the Only Monosemous Words.

3) WSD using dependency relations with the target word: In this WSD system, we employ word embeddings of the words that have direct dependency relations with the target word. We extract co-occurrence words that have dependency relations with the target word and represent their word embeddings. We calculate the average of word embeddings of their co-occurrence words. Then, a WSD classifier for the target word is constructed from a training set of the average vectors of input sentences and their appropriate sense label (Figure 3).

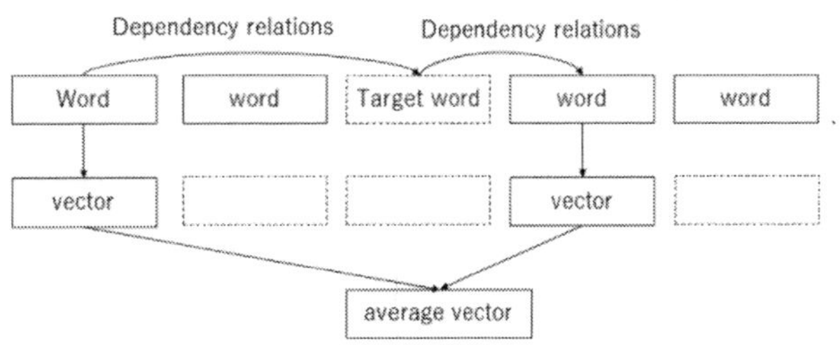

Fig. 3. WSD Using Dependency Relations with the Target word.

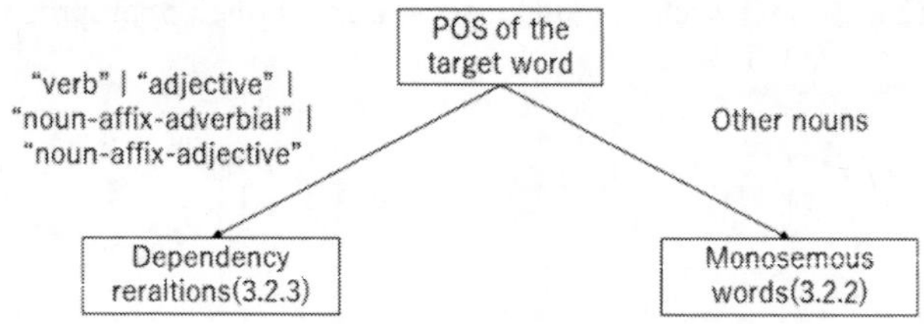

Fig. 4. WSD Using Both of Two Methods.

TABLE I
EXPERIENTIALE RESULTS OF APPLYING THE FOUR METHODS

Methods	Ave. Precision
Baseline (3.3.1)	70.16%
Monosemous (3.3.2)	68.40%
Dependency (3.3.3)	70.56%
Mono+Dep (3.3.4)	**72.08%**

4) WSD using both of the above two methods: In this WSD method, we use both of the above two methods. According to the part-of-speech of the target word, we select which method to use from the above methods. If the part of speech of the target word is "verb", "adjective", "noun-affix-adverbial" or "noun-affix-adjective", we use the WSD method that mentioned in the Section III-B2. If the part of speech of the target word is the other nouns, we use the WSD method that mentioned in the Section III-B3 (Figure 4).

IV. Experiments

To evaluate the efficiency of the proposed WSD method using word embeddings of the monosemous words in context and word dependency, we conduct some experiments to compare with the result of the baseline system. In this section, we describe an outline of the experiments.

A. Data Set

We use the Semeval-2010 Japanese WSD task data set, which includes 50 target words comprising 22 nouns, 23 verbs, and 5 adjectives [10]. In this data set, there are 50 training and 50 test instances for each target word.

B. Word Vector Representations

In these experiments, we use the two available pre-trained Japanese word embeddings. The first set of word vectors is "nwjc2vec" [12]. The nwjc2vec is pre-trained word embeddings constructed from NINJAL Web Japanese Corpus using word2vec. The second set is "Asahi Shimbun Word Vectors"[1]. This set is constructed from about 8 millions newspaper articles from Asahi Shimbun, which is a Japanese newspaper.

C. Preprocessing

Semantic and Syntactic features are extracted from the context of the target word (two words to the right and left) as described in the previous section. Each sentence of training data and test data is segmented into words by a morphological analyzer. As a morphological analyzer, we use MeCab[3] to obtain words and their part-of-speech. To obtain dependency relations for all words in a sentence, we use Cabocha[2] as a syntactic analyzer. Moreover, to improve performance, we remove words used as noun suffix and affix, and Japanese stop words from context words, such as "こと (thing)" and " 様 (like)", etc.

For the obtained feature set of training data, we construct classification model using Support Vector Machine (SVM). When the classification model is obtained, we predict one sense for each test example using this model. To employ the SVM for distinguishing more than two senses, we use one-versus-rest binary classication approach for each sense. As a result of the classification, we obtain precision value of each method to analyze the average performance of systems.

TABLE II
EXPERIENTIAL RESULTS OF APPLYING THE THREE TYPES OF WORD EMBEDDINGS.

Vectors	Baseline	Mono+Dep(3.3.4)
asahi(skip-gram)	69.52%	**70.04%**
asahi(cbow)	69.16%	**69.96%**
asahi(glove)	69.20%	**70.60%**
nwjc2vec	70.16%	**72.08%**

D. Experimental Results

Table I shows the results of the experiments of applying the four methods in the previous section. According this table, the proposed methods using word embeddings of the only monosemous words and using dependency relations with the target word achieve better results than the baseline system. However, the WSD method using word embeddings of the only monosemous words does not achieve improvement over the baseline system. As the results of these experiments, word embeddings of the monosemous words are effective for noun word sense disambiguation task except for noun-common-adverb and noun-adjective-base form. If the target word is verb, adjective and noun (noun-common-adverb and noun-adjective-base form), word embedding features of co-occurrence words are not so effective to capture the characteristics of context.

Regardless of the part-of-speech of the target word, word embeddings of the words that have direct dependency relations with the target word are effective to obtain context information. In this way, by selecting the WSD method according to the part-of-speech of the target word, we consider that the average precision of the all target words can be increased.

Moreover, we now show that the proposed method can be applied to other word embeddings. To do so, we use a word embedding based on the "Asahi Shimbun Word Vectors". Table II shows the results of the experiments of applying the three types of word embeddings in the "Asahi Shimbun Word Vectors" (skip-gram, CBOW and GloVe). The proposed methods using these word embeddings achieve better results than the baseline system. However, the average precision of the WSD system slightly decreased in compared with the method using nwjc2vec.

V. Conclusion and Future Work

In this paper, we proposed a new method for WSD using word embeddings of the monosemous words in context and word dependency. The efficiency of the proposed method was evaluated on the Semeval-2010 Japanese WSD task dataset. The results showed that the proposed methods using word embeddings of the only monosemous words and using dependency relations with the target word achieve better results than the baseline system.

In the future, we will analyze the dependency relation and the co-occurrence relation between monosemous words and polysemous words to investigate the effectiveness of monosemous words for word sense disambiguation. Moreover, for providing more useful sense information, we will construct a lexical semantic resource which is useful for expressing the target relation of monosemous words.

References

[1] "Asahi shimbun word vectors," http://www.asahi.com/shimbun/medialab/word_embedding/, [accessed October 2018].

[2] "Cabocha: Yet another japanese dependency structure analyzer," http://taku910.github.io/cabocha/, [accessed October 2018].

[3] "Mecab: Yet another part-of-speech and morphological analyzer," http://taku910.github.io/mecab/, [accessed October 2018].

[4] X. Chen, Z. Liu, and M. Sun, "A unified model for word sense representation and disambiguation," in *Proceedings of the 2014 Conference on Empirical Methods in Natural Language Processing (EMNLP)*. Association for Computational Linguistics, 2014, pp. 1025–1035.

[5] P. Kathuria and K. Shirai, "Word sense disambiguation based on example sentences in dictionary and automatically acquired from parallel corpus," in *Proceedings of the Advances in Natural Language Processing: 8th International Conference on NLP (JapTAL2012)*, H. Isahara and K. Kanzaki, Eds. Berlin, Heidelberg: Springer Berlin Heidelberg, 2012, pp. 210–221.

[6] J. Li and C. Huang, "A model for word sense disambiguation," in *International Journal of Computational Linguistics & Chinese Language Processing, Volume 4, Number 2, August 1999*, 1999, pp. 1–20.

[7] T. Mikolov, I. Sutskever, K. Chen, G. Corrado, and J. Dean, "Distributed representations of words and phrases and their compositionality," in *Proceedings of the 26th International Conference on Neural Information Processing Systems - Volume 2*, ser. NIPS'13. USA: Curran Associates Inc., 2013, pp. 3111–3119.

[8] K. Nagamatsu and H. Tanaka, "Evaluation of a similarity measure based on co-occurrence and dependency between words," in *Technical report of the Special Interest Group on Natural Language Processing of the Information Processing Society in Japan (IPSJ-NL) (in Japanese)*, vol. 116-11, 1996.

[9] R. Navigli, "Word sense disambiguation: A survey," *ACM Computing Surveys*, vol. 41, no. 2, pp. 10:1–10:69, Feb. 2009.

[10] M. Okumura, K. Shirai, K. Komiya, and H. Yokono, "Semeval-2010 task: Japanese wsd," in *Proceedings of the 5th International Workshop on Semantic Evaluation*, ser. SemEval '10. Stroudsburg, PA, USA: Association for Computational Linguistics, 2010, pp. 69–74.

[11] M. Sasaki, K. Komiya, and H. Shinnou, "Efficiency of the dictionary definition for word sense disambiguation based on word embeddings," in *22nd Annual Meeting of the Association of Natural Language Processing (in Japanese)*, 2016, pp. 449–452.

[12] H. Shinnou, M. Asahara, K. Komiya, and M. Sasaki, "nwjc2vec: Word embedding data constructed from ninjal web japanese corpus," in *Journal of Natural Language Processing*, vol. 24-5, 2017, pp. 705–720.

[13] H. Sugawara, H. Takamura, R. Sasano, and M. Okumura, "Context representation with word embeddings for wsd," in *Computational Linguistics: 14th International Conference of the Pacific Association for Computational Linguistics, PACLING 2015*. Singapore: Springer Singapore, 2015, pp. 108–119.

[14] D. Yarowsky, "Unsupervised word sense disambiguation rivaling supervised methods," in *Proceedings of the 33rd Annual Meeting on Association for Computational Linguistics*, ser. ACL '95. Stroudsburg, PA, USA: Association for Computational Linguistics, 1995, pp. 189–196.

An Ontology for Cultural Heritage Protection against Climate Change

Jürgen Moßgraber
Fraunhofer IOSB
Karlsruhe, Germany
juergen.mossgraber@iosb.fraunhofer.de

Paraskevi Pouli
Foundation for Research and Technology - Hellas
Heraklion, Greece
ppouli@iesl.forth.gr

Désirée Hilbring
Fraunhofer IOSB
Karlsruhe, Germany
desiree.hilbring@iosb.fraunhofer.de

Guiseppina Padeletti
Consiglio Nazionale delle Ricerche, ISMN
Rome, Italy
pad@mlib.cnr.it

Tobias Hellmund
Fraunhofer IOSB
Karlsruhe, Germany
tobias.hellmund@iosb.fraunhofer.de

Abstract—**Environmental factors, worsened by the increasing climate change impact, represent significant threats to European Cultural Heritage (CH) assets. In Europe, the huge number and diversity of CH assets, together with the different climatological sub-regions aspects, as well as the different adaptation policies to climate change adopted (or to be adopted) by the different nations, generate a very complex scenario. This paper will present a multidisciplinary methodology that will bridge the gap between two different worlds: the CH stakeholders and the scientific/technological experts. Since protecting cultural heritage assets and increasing their resilience against effects caused by the climate change is a multidisciplinary task, experts from many domains need to work together to meet their conservation goals. This paper discusses a method for facilitating the work for the different experts. A new ontology has been designed integrating all necessary aspects for improving the resilience of cultural heritages on site. This ontology combines the following topics: Cultural Heritage Assets, Stakeholders and Roles, Climate and Weather Effects, Risk Management, Conservation Actions, Materials, Sensors, Models and Observations, Standard Operation Procedures/Workflows and Damages.**

Keywords - Ontology; Knowledge Base; Ontology Visualization; Cultural Heritage.

I. INTRODUCTION

Europe has a significant cultural diversity together with exceptional historic architectures and artefact collections that attract millions of tourists every year. These incalculable values and global assets have to be preserved for future generations. Environmental factors, worsened by the increasing climate change impact, represent significant threats to CH assets such as monuments, historic structures and settlements, places of worship, cemeteries and archaeological sites. There are almost 400 UNESCO sites in Europe, located in different climatic European regions [1][2].

Therefore, eco-compatible solutions and materials for the long-term sustainable maintenance and preservation of CH in response to the events induced by climate changes are a necessity. The research and development of these solutions will benefit from an Information and Communication platform able to provide a timely up-to-date situational awareness about the site, thus supporting decision makers to plan the actions necessary for long term and short-term maintenance, intervention and risk management against the threats of the climate change. Life cycle assessment of the interventions on CH will be performed as comparative methodology supporting the decision making process.

Section 2, "Related Work" discusses Information and Communication Technologies (ICT) and existing ontologies and vocabularies in the CH domain. Section 3, "The HERACLES Project" introduces the project in which the ontology is developed and used in a Knowledge Base (KB) including two testbed case studies. Section 4 presents the creation and content of the HERACLES ontology. Since not all aspects can be covered in this paper, the focus lies on risk management, sensors, models, assets, materials and response actions. Finally Section 5, "Conclusions and Future Work" recapitulates our findings and discusses directions for future developments.

II. RELATED WORK

During the last 20 years, there has been an increasing interest and demand for specialized scientific technologies and methodologies in the CH field. An increasing number of experts from different scientific disciplines, such as curators, archaeologists, conservators, art historians, scientists and engineers, are involved in the analysis and study of CH assets and monuments, each one of them using his own specialized terminology. To overcome the communication gap among the CH experts, it is important to develop tools able to solve this issue. Information and Communication Technologies can support this interdisciplinary research [3].

Firstly, electronic handbooks, web-based knowledge platforms together with mobile phone applications, expert and decision support systems have been developed to improve the handling of the data and to promote the dissemination and a better understanding of the scientific information from the technical investigations. Above all, these ICTs facilitate the cooperation between CH experts. Two examples of Web knowledge tools, platforms and applications, developed by CH organizations and museums, are the following:

- An interactive website by the TATE Gallery presents information about the artworks identity, the materials, the structure and the construction technology, the description of the conservation steps, the investigation procedures, the results and the assessment of their condition state [4].
- Diadrasis, a nonprofit organization, has developed an online application entitled Viaduct [5], which classifies and explains a number of analysis and dating methods and provides basic information about the investigation methods and the related glossary.

In parallel, a correct and controlled terminology has become particularly important in the electronic documentation and presentation of the assets and of their restoration. In this respect, a number of thesauri, terminology glossaries, vocabularies and databases have been introduced, for example:

- The Art & Architecture Thesaurus (AAT) is a structured vocabulary used to improve the understanding of the terms about art, architecture, and material culture [6].
- The European illustrated glossary of conservation terms for wall paintings and architectural surfaces (EwaGlos) is an illustrated glossary of conservation terms translated in eleven languages. The core of the glossary includes approximately 200 definitions of the terms frequently used in the field of the conservation/restoration of the wall paintings and of the architectural surfaces [7].
- NARCISSE, an European project, has developed a very high-resolution image bank, dedicated to the art treasures of Europe major museums. A multilingual glossary of terms about the conservation of paintings, illustrated with various spectral images, was developed [8].
- POLYGNOSIS is a web-based knowledge platform, designed and implemented with an educational orientation, concerning the optical and laser-based investigation methods for the study of CH objects [9]. POLYGNOSIS handles information related to the analysis of the studied materials and in this respect it offers an important background for the HERACLES ontology regarding the characterization of materials.

The design process of the HERACLES ontology included the research and analysis of existing ontologies.

The CIDOC Conceptual Reference Model (CRM) is a model, which provides definitions and a formal structure for describing the concepts and relationships used in cultural heritage documentation [10]. CIDOC CRM can be extended with additional models, such as the CRM scientific observation model, or the CRM model for archeological buildings.

However, so far, no attempts have been undertaken to model the risks and the effects of climate change on CH buildings and monuments, the caused damage and the materials most suitable for restoration. We fear that the inclusion of missing ontological concepts like weather phenomena, risk analysis and crisis management into the already existing models will result in added levels of complexity to the existing ontologies. Therefore, the approach followed in HERACLES has been to create a new ontological model from scratch trying to keep it as concise as possible. The ontology has been developed in a workshop with stakeholders of the project with in-depth domain knowledge background, as described by Moßgraber et al. [11]. Hereby, it incorporates all domains that are relevant for the end-users. The following sources have been used as reference material for the new ontology: the SWEET ontologies developed at the NASA Jet Propulsion Laboratory [12], the materials ontology from Ashino [13] and Open Geospatial Consortium (OGC) standards such as the SensorThing Application Programming Interface (API) [14] and the Internet of Things (IoT) Tasking Capability [15].

III. THE HERACLES PROJECT

The main objective of the HERACLES project is to design, validate and promote responsive systems and solutions for effective resilience of CH against climate change effects, considering as mandatory premise a holistic, multidisciplinary approach through the involvement of different expertise (end-users, industry, scientists, conservators, restorators and social experts, decision, and policy makers) [16]. This will be pursued with the development of a system exploiting an ICT platform able to collect and integrate multisource information. With the help of this platform, complete and updated awareness is provided. It will also facilitate the integration of innovative measurements improving CH resilience, including new solutions for maintenance and conservation [17]. The validation is executed in four test sites, namely Heraklion in Crete with the Minoan Palace of Knossos and the Venetian Sea Fortress of Koules and Gubbio in Italy with Consoli Palace and the town walls. These test beds represent key study cases for the climate change impact on European CH assets. The strength of HERACLES solutions is their flexibility in evaluating a large quantity of different pieces of information utilized via explicit semantic modelling tailored to the specific CH assets needs. In this context, end-users play a fundamental role. Through consequent end-user focus, we aim to develop a complete, yet flexible system that is able to embrace other test-beds as well. End-users have an active part in the project activities and have permanent access to the

HERACLES KB, which implements the HERACLES ontology presented in this paper. Through the ontology, the stored and retrieved knowledge from the KB is language independent.

IV. Design of the HERACLES Ontology

As outlined in the section "Related Work" we decided to create a new concise ontology model. To identify the ontological classes and relations, a workshop was held, which brought together all stakeholders of the project with their different research and domain knowledge backgrounds. This group consisted of about 20 persons. For a workshop, this number is considered too large, but was necessary due to the different required domains.

Stakeholders could assist during the design process of the ontology through an easy to use online collaboration tool with graphical ontology visualization and functions to facilitate the creation of instances (Figures 1 and 2).

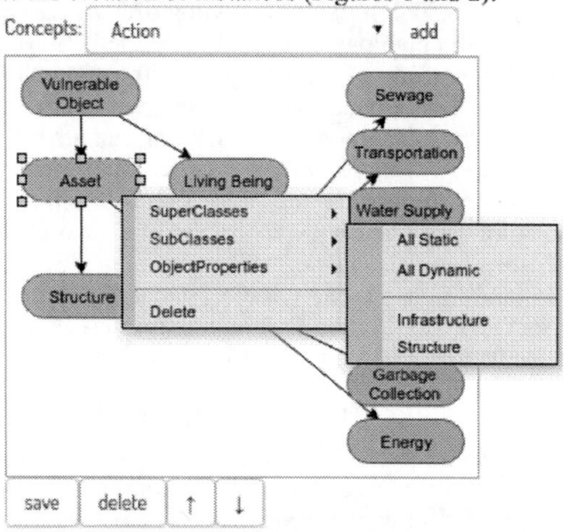

Figure 1. Tool with graphical ontology visualisation

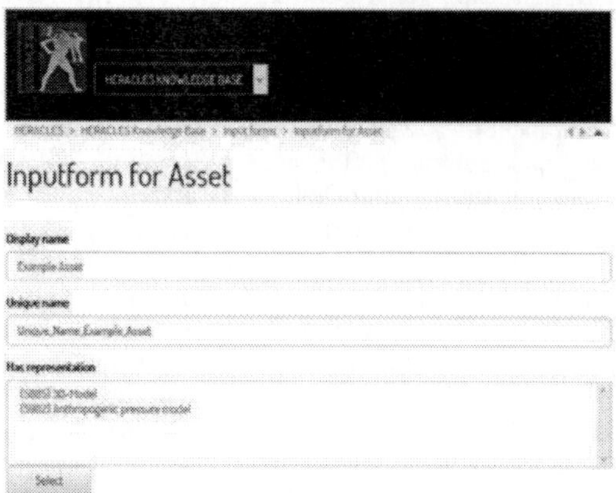

Figure 2. Instance creation

The following graphical conventions are used for the description of the HERACLES ontology:

- Green boxes represent concepts; grey boxes represent instances.
- Continuous arrows represent semantic relationships between concepts or instances. Inverse relationships are omitted for better readability. A label next to an arrow describes the relationship.
- Dashed arrows link subclasses to parent classes.
- Dotted arrows link instances to their concepts.

Concepts in the ontology are accompanied by attributes (datatype properties). For example, an asset can have geographical coordinates or a construction period. For the sake of brevity, these are omitted in the ontology pictures.

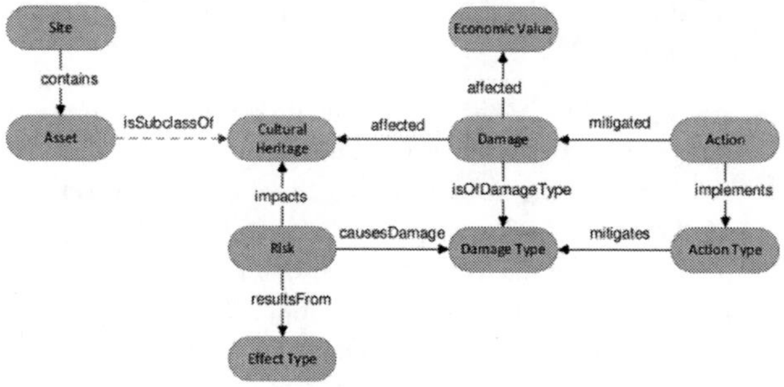

Figure 3. The main concepts and their object properties of the HERACLES ontology.

The central elements in the ontology are the CH assets that need to be protected against the effects of climate change. As shown in Figure 3, a top-level class is defined to refer to any kind of CH. Risks arise from climate change effects which can cause damages to CH. As seen in Figure 3, a distinction is made between types of potential damage ("Damage Type") and actual damage ("Damage"). The system also records potential mitigation actions and actual performed actions.

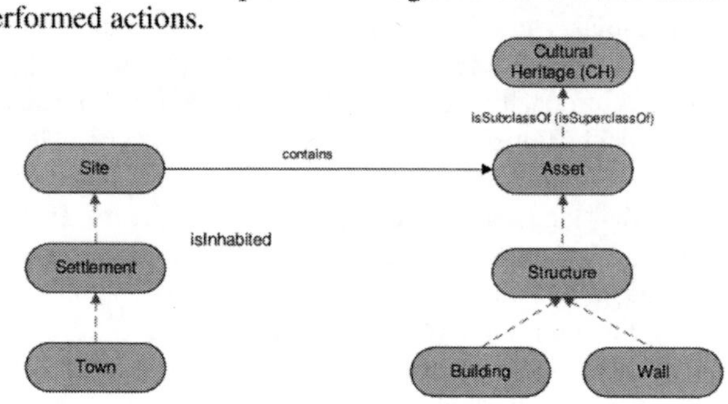

Figure 4. Cultural Heritage Asset

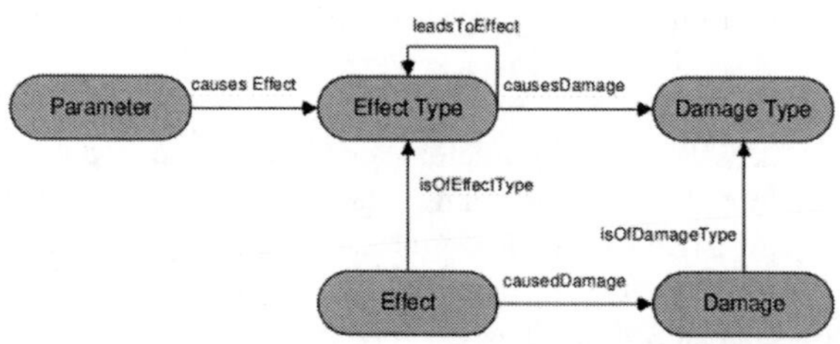

Figure 5. From effect to damage, distinction between potential and actual fact

A. *Cultural Heritage Assets*

Assets, which are the focus of the project, are a subclass of CH. The Asset concept is further refined with the concept Structure and, below that, Monument, Building or Wall (see Figure 4). Via these classes, the actual instances of the test beds of the HERACLES project, like the "Knossos Palace", the "Palazzo dei Consoli", the "Venetian Fortification" and the "Gubbio Townwall", can be included.

Assets are located in Sites, which are classified into more specialized classes like a Settlement.

B. *Climate Change Effects*

In Figure 5, the distinction between potential, meaning things that may occur and facts, in the sense of actual occurrences, is emphasized. This distinction applies to effects ("Effect Type" vs. "Effect") and damage. As an example, the ontology may contain flood as a potential effect type that may damage an asset. Besides that, the flood episodes that occurred in specific years are also registered as actual occurrences in the KB. The ontology contains the relationships between potential effects ("Effect Type"), follow-up potential effects ("leadsToEffect") and the potential damage ("Damage Type") they may cause. An example with instances for the classes shown in Figure 5 is given in Figure 6. Heavy Precipitation can lead to a Landslide. If such a Landslide hits an asset, it can result in Structural Damage. A specific event is shown below these generic types: A heavy precipitation episode occurred at a specific date and time, which caused a landslide in a specific area, which hits a wall and destroys it.

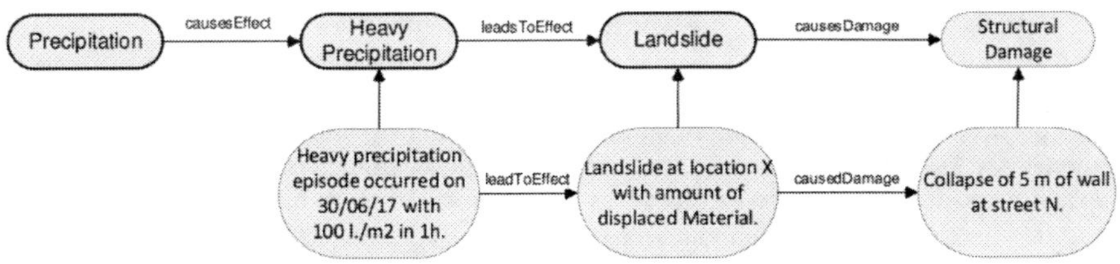

Figure 6. Example for effects and caused damage and their types.

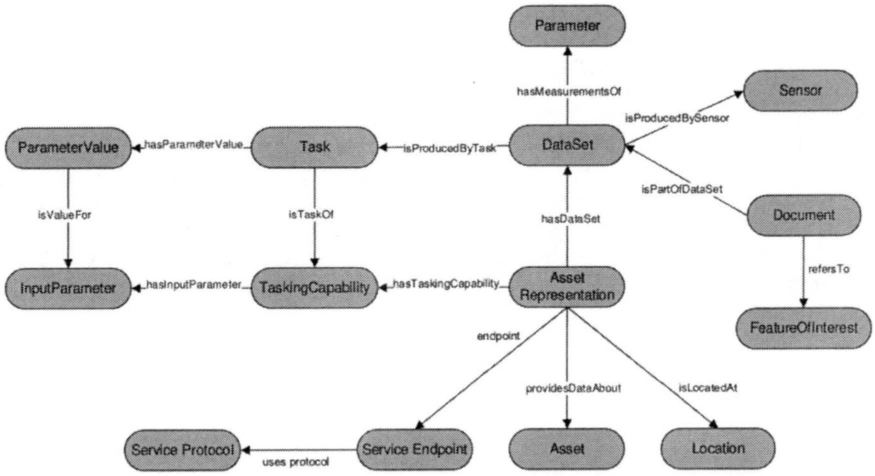

Figure 7. Classes for managing metadata of sensors, models and measurement campaigns.

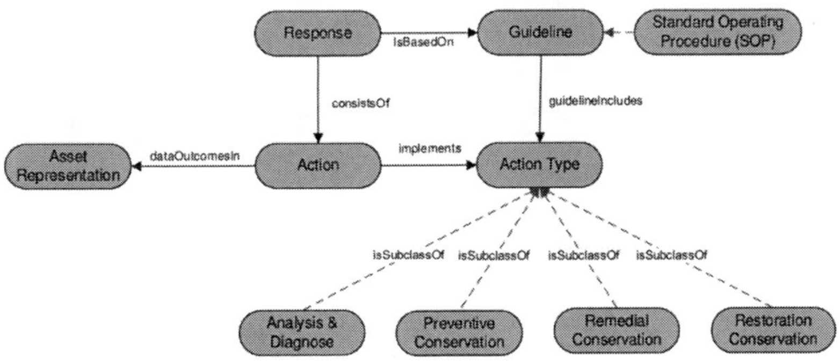

Figure 8. Maintenance and response actions.

C. *Sensors and Simulation models*

To capture climate change relevant parameters, sensors were modelled according to the SensorThings API standard, which was presented by the OGC [14]. The SensorThings API is a modern standard for providing an open and unified way to connect IoT devices, data and applications over the Web [15]. Therefore, the initial design of the ontology classes for dealing with sensor metadata is based on the data model of the SensorThings API standard. It is reasonable to follow the same standard for developing the ontology for simulation models. In practice, requesting the execution of a model is equivalent to tasking an actuator to perform a particular task but, since the tasking part of SensorThings API was not yet available, it is not considered in the paper. For this reason, the adaptation of the ontology is based on the "Internet of Things Tasking Capability" [16], in which an extension of the SensorThings API for tasking actuators is proposed.

The central concept in the diagram (see Figure 7) is the "Asset Representation". An Asset Representation is an entity that provides data about an asset. It can be regarded as a proxy that enables access to the available data about an asset, for example, temperatures in a building, images and measurements of the building obtained in a measurement campaign or the results from a structural model. The actual sensor measurement is stored in an observation, which is connected to a data stream. The four classes on the left in Figure 7: TaskingCapability, Task, InputParameter and ParameterValue, provide support to store and manage metadata about the models. The TaskingCapability provides a human-readable description of the model together with information regarding the API that the model provides. In the HERACLES platform, there is an additional abstraction layer, namely the KB, which manages the metadata of the available models and sensors.

D. *Maintenance and Response Actions*

Situational awareness is achieved through continuous monitoring of the status of the CH assets combined with the results provided by the simulation models, which enable risk assessment. Evaluation of the information provided by the system and on-the-field observations enable the identification of actual or potential problems, for instance, when a risk level threshold is trespassed or a damage is observed. The modeling of such problems has been included in the ontology.

Maintenance actions not related to an issue also need to be documented. In this way, the structure of the ontology can serve as a register of past actions that can be used to better understand the current situation and support the decision making process. Suggested actions are documented in formalized guidelines, which are often supported by a specific law; these are the Standard Operating Procedures (SOPs) (see Figure 8).

E. *Materials*

Since materials have an influence on how an asset is affected by climate effects in terms of its resilience to weathering and ageing, it is important that the ontology also models information about materials and the KB contains information about materials and of which materials an asset consists of. The material area can be ground for experimentation of new solutions to be applied for maintenance and restoration/conservation of CH assets.

The classes to keep materials information in the KB are provided in Figure 9. The level of detail regarding the information about the composition, structure and properties of the materials needs further discussion with both materials experts and end users. Nevertheless, it should be noted that some ontologies associated with the handling of material related information already exist [10]. Whereas the detail of such specialized ontologies may be too excessive for its application in our use cases, they provide a reference to develop a model for the HERACLES platform. At the same time, since the aforementioned ontologies are not designed with a specific application field in mind, extra classes and properties may be necessary in the HERACLES platform for its utilization in the context of CH conservation.

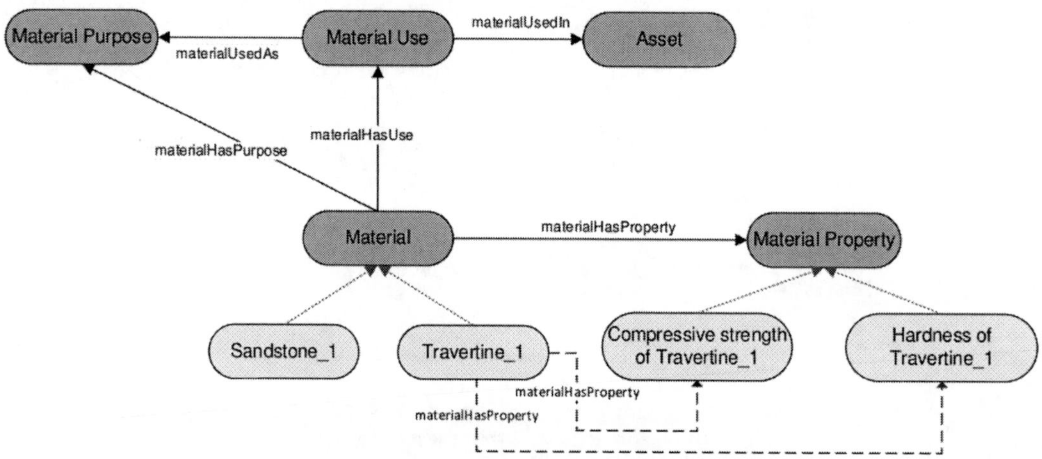

Figure 9. Classes keeping material information

F. *Ontology Metrics*

This section provides the metrics of the current state of the HERACLES ontology. It includes *general* metrics like the number of classes, data/objects properties and individuals and *annotation axioms* like the numbers of annotation property. Inverse properties are excluded in this listing (see Table 1).

TABLE I. ONTOLOGY METRICS

Metric	Value
Class count	109
Object property count	102
Data properties count	49
Individual count	141

V. CONCLUSIONS AND FUTURE WORK

This paper presented the design of the HERACLES ontology, which aggregates multiple domains and therefore, required the interaction of multiple domain experts. Using a tool, which supports online collaboration with graphical ontology visualization, creation of input forms, etc. speeds up this process. The ontology is the basis for further research projects, which need to tackle the problems of climate change effects and involve a set of heterogeneous sensors and processing algorithms. Furthermore, it can be used as basis for the suggestion of materials that comply with historic building materials and can be used to restore the structural health of cultural heritage assets. Apart from future possibilities, the ontology offers functionalities that are already in use: the consolidation of information describing the situation at a cultural heritage site rises situational awareness and the graphic display of concepts serves as full-fletched and navigable glossary for the project partners.

Besides the various additions to the ontology model discussed above, further work will be performed to fill the Knowledge Base using the developed ontology. Additionally, research will focus on the reasoning techniques, which will be applied to the semantic data to automatically suggest necessary preservation actions. Another imminent step is to have end-users evaluating the ontology-based decision support providing possible recommendations. This assessment will take place in a few months' time, when the first pilot deployments will be evaluated in the field. Action will also be taken on mapping concepts from the HERACLES ontology to other prominent models, like the CIDOC-RM, to guarantee interoperability and facilitate the ontology's reuse.

The ontology has been published here [18], where the interested reader is encouraged to examine the ontology.

ACKNOWLEDGMENT

This project has received funding from the European Union's Horizon 2020 research and innovation program under grant agreement No 700395.

REFERENCES

[1] UNESCO, Climate Change and World Heritage, world heritage reports 22, http://whc.unesco.org/documents/publi_wh_papers_22_en.pdf last accessed 2018/11/08

[2] UNESCO, Table Principal Climate Change risks and impacts on cultural heritage, WHC-06/30.COM/7.1, http://whc.unesco.org/archive/2006/whc06-30com-07.1e.doc, last accessed 2018/11/08

[3] M. Doerr, "Ontologies for Cultural Heritage," in Handbook on Ontologies, International Handbooks on Information Systems 19, pp. 463-486, Springer, 2009.

[4] TATE Gallery Homepage, http://www.tate.org.uk, last accessed 2018/09/21.

[5] S. Blain, A. Dimitrakopoulou, L. Gomez-Robles and L. Tapini, "Viaduct, a communication tool for scientific analysis in heritage", ISBN 978-618-81473-1-7, Diadrasis, 2015.

[6] AAT (Art & Architecture Thesaurus Online) Homepage, The Getty Research Institute, The J. Paul Getty Trust, Los Angeles (USA). http://www.getty.edu/research/tools/vocabularies/aat/, last accessed 2018/09/21.

[7] A. Weyer et. al. (eds.), "EwaGlos-European Illustrated Glossary of Conservation Terms for Wall Paintings and Architectural Surfaces," ISBN: 978-3-7319-0260-7, Michael Imhof Verlag, Petersberg, Germany, 2015.

[8] C. Lahanier and M. Aubert, "Network of art research computer image systems in Europe (NARCISSE)," Museums and interactive multimedia: proceedings of an international conference, pp. 298-304, Cambridge, England, 1993.

[9] N. Platia et. al, "POLYGNOSIS: the development of a thesaurus in an Educational Web Platform on optical and laser-based investigation methods for cultural heritage analysis and diagnosis," Heritage Science, 5 (50), 2017, Doi:10.1186/s40494-017-0163-0.

[10] P. Le Boeuf, M. Doerr, C. E. Ore and S. Stead, "Definition of the CIDOC conceptual reference model," ICOM/CIDOC Documentation Standards Group, 1999. www.cidoc-crm.org, last accessed 2018/09/21.

[11] J. Moßgraber, M. Schenk and D. Hilbring, "Modelling of an Ontology for a Communication Platform," Proceedings of The Ninth International Conference on Advances in Semantic Processing, pp. 97-102, Nice, France, 2015.

[12] R. G. Raskin and M. J. Pan, "Knowledge representation in the semantic web for Earth and environmental terminology (SWEET)," Computers & Geosciences, Vol. 31, pp. 1119 – 1125, 2005.

[13] T. Ashino, "Materials ontology: An infrastructure for exchanging materials information and knowledge," Data Science Journal, Vol. 9, pp. 54-61, 2010.

[14] S. Liang, C.-Y. Huang and T. Khalafbeigi, OGC SensorThings API, Open Geospatial Consortium: Wayland, MA, USA, 2016.

[15] C.-Y. Huang and C.-H. Wu, "A Web Service Protocol Realizing Interoperable Internet of Things Tasking Capability," Sensors, Vol. 16(9), 1395, Basel, Switzerland, 2016.

[16] HERACLES Homepage, http://www.heracles-project.eu/, last accessed 2018/09/21.

[17] J. Moßgraber, G. Lortal, F. Calabrò and M. Corsi, "An ICT Platform to support Decision Makers with Cultural Heritage Protection against Climate Events," Geophysical Research Abstracts, Vol. 20, p. 13962, Vienna, Austria, 2018.

[18] Fraunhofer IOSB: https://github.com/FraunhoferIOSB/HERACLES, last accessed 2018/11/08

A Survey of Ontology Learning from Text

Kaoutar Belhoucine and Mohammed Mourchid
MISC laboratory, Faculty of Science
Ibn Tofail University
Kenitra, Morocco
e-mail: kaouar.belhoucine@gmail.com, mourchidm@hotmail.com

Abstract—**Ontologies are considered to be a major solution to semantic interoperability in modern information systems. The explosion of textual information on the Web and advanced state in related fields, such as Natural Language Processing (NLP), information retrieval, and data mining, have made (semi-) automatic ontology learning from text a particularly promising research area. This article summarizes the state-of-the-art in ontology learning from text, and discusses the research questions and challenges that remain in this field.**

Keywords-Ontology Learning from Text; Ontology Learning Layer Cake Model; Ontology Evaluation; Trends; Challenges.

I. Introduction

Ontologies constitute an approach for knowledge representation that defines concepts and their relationships, constraints, axioms, and the vocabulary of a given domain. An ontology should be machine understandable (which excludes natural language), and should capture the consensual knowledge, that is not private to an individual, but accepted by a group as committee of practice.

Ontologies are of great importance to modern knowledge-based systems. By providing a shared schema, they facilitate query answering and reasoning over disparate data sources. However, the manual construction of ontologies is a difficult and expensive task that usually requires a collaboration between domain experts and skilled ontology engineers. Even then, once the ontology has been constructed, our evolving knowledge and updated application requirements demand a process of continuous maintenance on the ontology.

This difficulty in capturing the knowledge required by knowledge-based systems is called "knowledge acquisition bottleneck". To overcome this bottleneck, an automatic or semi-automatic support for ontology construction is desired. This area of research is usually referred to as ontology learning [1]-[3].

We present in this paper a survey of ontology learning from text. Section 2 introduces the ontology concept as it is considered in this discipline. Section 3 discusses the overall process of ontology learning from text: inputs, approaches, techniques, and prominent ontology learning systems. Evaluation methods for ontology learning are discussed in Section 4. Finally, Section 5 concludes with a final discussion on the contemporary trends and remaining challenges in the field.

II. Ontologies

Before defining the process of ontology learning from text, we must first clarify what we mean by the term "ontology." The term "ontology" comes from the branch of philosophy that is concerned with the study of being or existence. However, within the discipline of Artificial Intelligence, scholars, such as T. Gruber define an ontology as a formal specification of the concepts of the domain of interest, where their relationships, constraints, and axioms are expressed, thus defining a common vocabulary for sharing knowledge [4]. Indeed, these two interdisciplinary definitions are complementary; what must be represented in a knowledge-based system is what exists. In other words, an ontology is composed of two parts; the first part consisting of concepts, taxonomic relations (relations which define a conceptual hierarchy) and of the non-taxonomic relations between them. Further, the other part is constructed of conceptual instances and assertions about them. More formally, an ontology can be defined, according to [5][6], as a tuple:

$$\vartheta := (C, H^C, R, rel, A^\vartheta). \quad (1)$$

Where:

- C is the set of ontology concepts. The concepts represent the entities of the domain being modeled. They are designated by one or more natural language terms and are normally referenced inside the ontology by a unique identifier.
- $H^C \subseteq C \times C$ is a set of taxonomic relationships between the concepts. Such relationships define the concept hierarchy.
- R is the set of non-taxonomic relationships.
- The function rel: $R \rightarrow C \times C$ maps the relation identifiers to the actual relationships.
- A^ϑ is a set of axioms, usually formalized into logic language. These axioms specify additional constraints on the ontology and can be used in ontology consistency checking, as well as inferring new knowledge from the ontology through an inference mechanism.

Besides these elements, there are also the instances of the concepts and relationships, e.g., the instances of the elements of C, H^C and R. A knowledge base is composed by an ontology ϑ and its instances.

III. Ontology Learning from Text

Ontology learning from text refers to the (semi)-automatic support for identifying concepts, relations, and (optionally) axioms from textual information and using them to first construct and, then, maintain an ontology. Techniques from established fields, such as information retrieval, data mining, and NLP, have all been fundamental in the development of ontology learning systems. This section examines the input used to learn ontologies, their learning approaches, their techniques, and the most prominent ontology learning systems.

A. The input used to learn ontologies

Ontology learning requires input data from which to learn the concepts relevant for any given domain and their definitions, as well as the relationships between them. Dominik Benz [7] defines three different kinds of ontology learning input data:

- Structured data: means data represented according to defined schema such as Database (DB) schemes, existing ontologies and knowledge bases.
- Semi-structured data: designates the use of some mixed structured data with free text, for example: dictionaries such as WordNet [9] or the Wiktionary [10], HTML and XML documents or Wikis and User Tags.
- Unstructured data: consists of natural language texts such as Word and PDF documents, or Web pages.

The term ontology learning from text is used if ontology learning is based on unstructured data [23]. This type of resources is the most available format as input for ontology learning processes. They reflect mostly the domain knowledge for which the user is building the ontology. In addition, they describe the terminology, concepts and conceptual structures of the given domain. However, some authors, such as M. Rogger et al. [11], consider that processing unstructured data is the most complicated problem because most of the knowledge is implicit and allows conceptualizing it by different people in different ways, even using the same words. For these reasons, this paper focuses especially on ontology learning from unstructured data.

B. Ontology learning approaches and techniques

As we have shown in the previous sections, ontology learning is primarily concerned with definition of concepts, relations, and (optionally) axioms from textual information and using them to construct and maintain an ontology. Although there is no standard regarding this development process, P. Cimiano [13] describes the tasks involved in ontology learning as forming a layer cake. As illustrated in Figure 1, the cake is composed, in ascending order, of terms, synonyms, concepts, taxonomies, relations, and, finally, axioms and rules. We shall now examine this cake layer by layer and present the different approaches and techniques used.

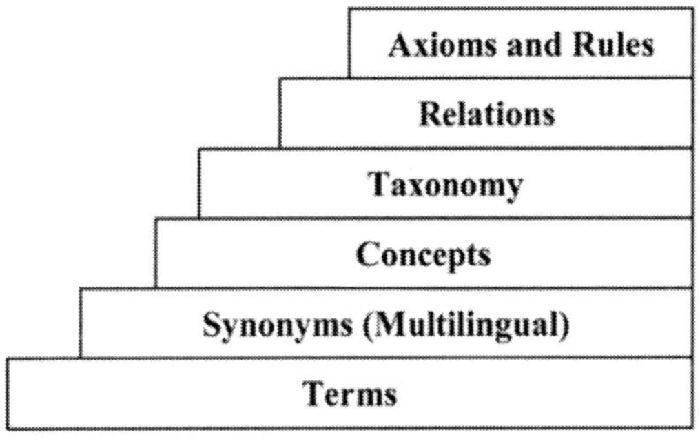

Figure 1. Ontology Learning "Layer Cake" [13].

1) Terms

Terms are the most basic building blocks of the ontology learning cake. Terms can be simple (i.e., single word) or complex (i.e., multi-word) and are considered as linguistic realizations of domain-specific concepts. There are many term extraction methods in ontology learning from text. Most of these extraction methods are based on terminology and NLP research [14]-[16], whilst others are based on information retrieval methods for term indexing [17]. The leading approaches of term extraction use tokenization (or part-of-speech tagging of the domain corpus) to identify terms by manually constructing ad-hoc patterns. Additionally, in order to identify only relevant term candidates, a statistical processing step may be used to compare the distribution of terms between domain specific and general corpora.

2) Synonyms

The synonyms layer addresses the acquisition of semantic term variants in and between languages. It is either based on sets, such as WordNet synsets [18] (after sense disambiguation), on clustering techniques [19]-[22] or other similar methods, including Web-based knowledge acquisition.

3) Concepts

Concepts can be abstract or concrete, real or fictitious. However, the consensus in this field is that concepts should include:

- Intension: formal definition of the set of objects that this concept describes.
- Extension: a set of objects that the definition of this concept describes.
- Lexical realizations: a set of linguistic realizations, (multilingual) terms for this concept.

Most of the research in concept extraction addresses the question from a clustering perspective, regarding concepts as clusters of related terms [13]. Obviously, this approach overlaps almost entirely with that of term and synonym extraction [23] and can be found in [24]-[27].

Alternatively, researchers have also addressed concept formation from an extensional point of view. For example, in the approach of [28][29], they derive hierarchies of named entities from text whilst also ascertaining concepts from an extensional point of view [13].

4) Concept Hierarchies (Taxonomy)

There are currently three main paradigms to induce concept hierarchies from textual data:

- The first one is the application of lexico-syntactic patterns to detect hyponymy relations, as proposed by [30]. However, it is well known that these patterns occur rarely in corpora. Consequently, though approaches relying on lexico-syntactic patterns have a reasonable degree of precision, their recall is very low.
- The second paradigm is based on Harris's distributional analysis [31]. In this paradigm, researchers have exploited clustering algorithms to automatically derive concept hierarchies from text.
- The third paradigm stems from the information retrieval community and relies on a document-based notion of term subsumption, as proposed for example in [32].

5) Relations (non-hierarchical)

Non-hierarchical relation extraction from text has been addressed primarily within the biomedical field, as there are a large text collections readily available for this area of research (e.g., PubMed [70]). The goal of this work is to discover new relationships between known concepts (i.e., symptoms, drugs, diseases, etc.) by analyzing large quantities of biomedical scientific articles (see e.g., [33]-[35]). Relation extraction through text mining for ontology development was introduced in work on association rules in [36]. Recent efforts in relation extraction from text have been carried on under the Automatic Content Extraction (ACE) program, where entities (i.e., individuals) are distinguished from their mentions. Normalization, the process of establishing links between mentions in a document, and individual entities represented in an ontology, is part of the task for certain kind of mentions (e.g., temporal expressions).

6) Axioms and rules

The extraction of rules from text occurs at an early stage [37]. Initial blueprints for this task can be found in the work of [38]. This work used an unsupervised method for discovering inference rules from the text, which was based on an extended version of the Harris' distributional hypothesis. Furthermore, the European Union-funded project Pascal [39] on textual entailment challenge has strongly increased the awareness of the problem of deriving lexical entailment rules. The focus of Pascal, therefore, was to learn lexical entailments for application in question answering systems.

C. *Prominent systems*

Several ontology learning systems have been proposed with the goal of reducing both the time and cost for ontology development. We present in this section the most prominent ontology learning systems according to the following criteria: broad adoption or popularity, completeness in the number of ontology learning tasks and outcomes, or recency of work.

- ASIUM [40] is a semi-automated ontology learning system that learns subcategorization frames of verbs and ontologies from syntactic parsing of technical texts in natural language (French). ASIUM successively aggregates the clusters to form new concepts in the form of a generality graph that represents the ontology of the domain.
- Text-to-Onto [21] is a framework for semi-automatic ontology learning from texts which implements a variety of algorithms for diverse ontology learning subtask. It leverages data mining and NLP techniques in the ontology development and maintenance task. It proceeds through ontology import, extraction, pruning, and refinement.
- SYNDIKATE [42] is a system for automatically acquiring knowledge from real-world texts, and for transferring their content to formal representation structures which constitute a corresponding text knowledge base. SYNDIKATE uses only linguistics-based techniques to perform its ontology learning tasks.
- OntoLearn [43] is a system for (semi-)automated ontology learning from domain texts. OntoLearn uses text mining techniques and existing linguistic resources, such as WordNet [9] and SemCor [69] to learn, from available document warehouses and dedicated Web sites, domain concepts and taxonomic relations among them.
- CRCTOL [44], known as Concept-Relation-Concept Tuple-based Ontology Learning, is a system to mine ontologies automatically from domain specific documents. CRCTOL uses linguistics and statistics-based techniques to perform its ontology learning tasks.
- OntoGain [22] is a system for unsupervised ontology acquisition from unstructured text which relies on multi-word term extraction. OntoGain uses linguistics and statistics-based techniques to perform its ontology learning tasks.
- OntoCmaps [58] is a domain-independent and ontology learning tool that extracts deep semantic representations from corpora. OntoCmaps generates rich conceptual representations in the form of concept maps and proposes an innovative filtering mechanism based on Degree (number of edges from and to a given term), Betweenness (number of shortest paths that pass through a term), PageRank (fraction of time spent visiting a term) and Hits (ranks terms according to the importance of hubs and authorities) metrics from graph theory.
- LexOnt [59] is a semi-automatic ontology creation tool that uses the Programmable Web directory of services. Its algorithm generates and ranks frequent terms and significant phrases by comparing them to external domain knowledge such as Wikipedia, WordNet and

the current state of the ontology. LexOnt constructs the ontology iteratively, by interacting with the user. The user can choose, add these terms to the ontology and rank terms.

Table I provides a comparison of the inputs used, outputs supported, and techniques employed by the prominent ontology learning systems from text.

TABLE I. SUMMARY OF PROMINENT ONTOLOGY LEARNING SYSTEMS FROM TEXT

System	Input Language	Input Type	Output	Technique		
				Linguistics-based	*Statistics-based*	*Logic-based*
ASIUM (2000)	French	Unstructured (corpora)	Terms Concepts	Sentence parsing, Syntactic Structure analysis, Subcategorization frames		
			Taxonomic relations		Agglomerative Clustering	
Text-to-Onto (2000)	German, XML, HTML, Document Type Definition (DTD)	Natural language texts, Web docs, semi-structured (XML, DTD) and structured (DB schema, ontology) data	Terms	Part-of-speech tagging, Sentence parsing, Syntactic Structure analysis		
			Concepts	Concepts from domain lexicon	Co-occurrence analysis	
			Taxonomic relations	Hypernyms from WordNet, Lexico-syntactic patterns	Agglomerative Clustering	
			Non-taxonomic relations		Association rule mining	
SYNDIKATE (2001)	German	Unstructured text	Terms	Syntactic Structure analysis, Anaphora resolution		
			Concepts	Use of semantic templates and domain knowledge		Inference engine
			Taxonomic relations			
			Non-taxonomic relations			
OntoLearn (2002)	French	Unstructured/semi structured text	Terms	Part-of-speech tagging, Sentence parsing	Relevance analysis	
			Concepts	Concepts and glossary from WordNet		
			Taxonomic relations	Hypernyms from WordNet		
CRCTOL (2005)	English	Unstructured/semi structured text (WordNet)	Terms and Concepts	Part-of-speech tagging, Sentence parsing, use of domain lexicon, Word sense disambiguation	Relevance analysis	
			Taxonomic and Non-taxonomic relations	Lexico-syntactic patterns, Syntactic Structure analysis		
OntoGain (2010)	English	Unstructured/semi structured text (WordNet)	Terms and Concepts	Part-of-speech tagging, Shallow parsing, Relevance analysis		
			Taxonomic relations		Agglomerative Clustering, Formal concept analysis	
			Non-taxonomic relations		Association rule mining	
OntoCmaps (2011)	English	Unstructured/semi structured text	Terms Concepts Taxonomic relations Non-taxonomic relations	Part-of-speech tagging and syntactic patterns based on dependency grammar formalism	Relevance analysis	
LexOnt (2012)	English	Unstructured, semi-structured (Wikipedia, WordNet) and structured (ontology) data	Terms Taxonomic relations	Linguistic patterns to determinate collocations	Relevance analysis	

As shown in Table I, most of the existing ontology learning systems focus only on concept and relation extraction. They generally rely on shallow NLP techniques and statistical methods. Though these systems are able to address the requirements of constructing small 'toy' ontologies, in time, the need for researchers to return to the basics and address more fundamental issues about knowledge acquisition bottleneck is revealed. This explains the reduction in the number of complete ontology learning systems developed in the last few years.

IV. Ontology Evaluation

"Ontology evaluation is defined in the context of two interesting concepts; verification and validation. The definition is interesting because it also offers a way to categorize current ontology evaluation endeavors. Ontology verification is concerned with building an ontology correctly, while ontology validation on the other hand is concerned with building the correct ontology" [61].

A. *Evaluation approaches*

A variety of approaches to ontology evaluation have been proposed in the literature [61][62][47]. Depending on the kind of ontology and the purpose of the evaluation, these approaches can be grouped into the following categories.

1) *Gold Standard-based evaluation*

Attempts to compare the learned ontology with a predefined gold standard ontology that represents an idealized outcome of the learning algorithm. However, having a suitable gold ontology can be challenging, since it should be one that was created under similar conditions with similar goals to the learned ontology [62].

2) *Task-based evaluation*

Examines how the results of the ontology-based application are affected by using the ontology [45]. For example, in the case of an ontology designed to improve the performance of document retrieval, users may collect some sample queries and determine if the documents retrieved are more relevant when the ontology is used.

3) *Corpus-based evaluation*

Evaluates how far an ontology is able to cover any given domain [45]. This type of approach compares the learned ontology with the content of a text corpus that significantly covers the corresponding domain. Techniques from natural language processing or information extraction are used to analyze the content of the corpus.

4) *Criteria-based evaluation*

Measures to what extent an ontology adheres to certain desirable criteria. We can distinguish between measures related to the structure of an ontology and more sophisticated measures [62].

B. *Evaluation tools*

Since the OntoWeb 2 position statement stressed the insufficient research on ontology evaluation and the lack of evaluation tools [48], several ontology evaluation tools have been developed. They differ according to the context of the evaluation. We present the most important examples below [12]:

- Swoogle [52] is an ontology search engine that offers a limited search facility that can be interpreted as topic coverage. Given a search keyword, Swoogle can retrieve ontologies that contain a class or a relation that (lexically) matches the given keyword.
- OntoKhoj [53] is an ontology search engine that extends the traditional (keyword-based search) approach to consider word senses when ranking ontologies covering any given topic. It accommodates a manual sense disambiguation process, then, according to the sense chosen by the user, hypernyms and synonyms are selected from WordNet.
- OntoQA [54] is a tool that measures the quality of ontology from the consumer perspective, using schema and instance metrics. It takes as an input a crawled populated ontology or a set of user supplied search terms, and ranks them according to metrics related to various aspects of an ontology.
- OntoCAT [55] provides a comprehensive set of metrics for use by the ontology consumer or knowledge engineer to assist in ontology evaluation for re-use. This evaluation process is focused on the ontology summaries that are based on size, structural, hub, and root properties.
- AKTiveRank [56] is a tool that ranks ontologies using a set of ontology structure-based metrics. It processes keywords as an input, and queries Swoogle for the given keywords in order to extract candidate ontologies. After that, it then applies measures based on the coverage and the structure of the ontologies to rank them accordingly. Its shortcoming is that its measures are at the "class level" only.
- OS_Rank [57] is an ontology evaluation system that evaluates ontologies and ranks them based on class name, the degree of detail for each searched class, the number of semantic relations of searched classes, and the interest domain based on WordNet to resolve different semantic problems.
- OOPS! (OntOlogy Pitfall Scanner!) [60] is a tool that scans ontologies looking for potential pitfalls that could led to modeling errors. OOPS! is very useful for ontology developers during the ontology validation activity, concretely during the diagnosis phase. The tool operates independently of any ontology development platform.

V. Ontology Learning Trends and Problems

To summarize the progress and trends that the ontology learning community has witnessed over the past years, we sent queries to Google Scholar, relating to ontology learning and compared the number of returned publications from 2007 to 2017. Some of our results are shown in Figure 2.

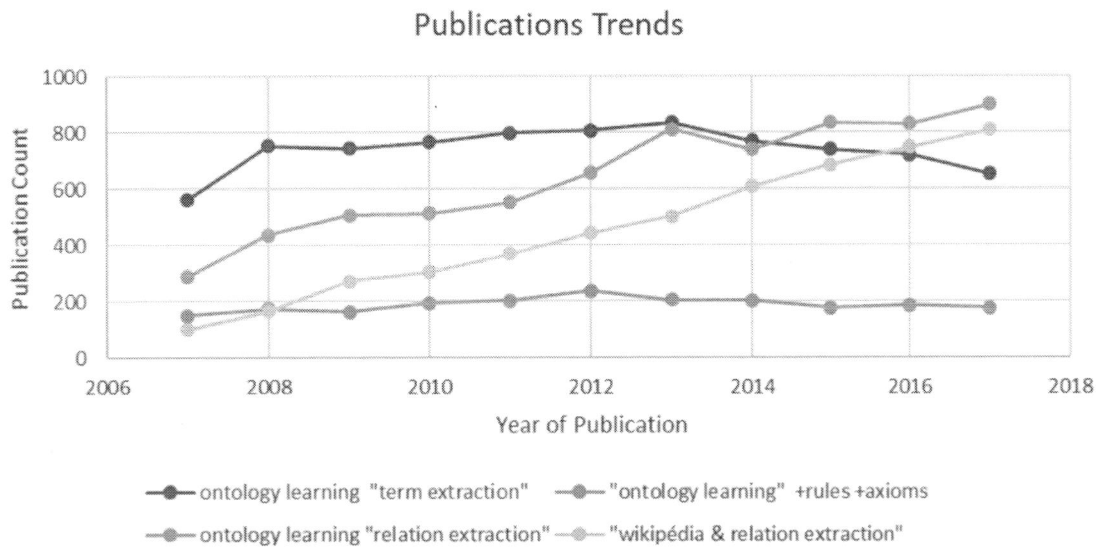

Figure 2. Publications Trends.

We browsed a large number of research papers that were returned. As a result of our research, we have observed the following trends:

- The most recent literature points to an increase in interest in using Web data to address the knowledge acquisition bottleneck and to make ontology learning operational on a Web scale.
- Current research efforts are focused on either enhancing existing term recognition techniques or moving to the more advanced phase of relation discovery.
- The measures of terms extraction from texts have more or less stabilized, with an F-measure generally above 90%. The current state-of-the-art techniques are based mainly on statistical semantics, and paradigmatic and syntagmatic relations [63] - that is to say, the relevance of search terms is determined through general observations in very large samples of data and through the way the constituent parts of the search term are constructed.
- There is a noticeable trend of increased application of lexico-syntactic patterns [64], machine learning methods [65], or hybrid approach that combines lexico-syntactic pattern analysis with supervised classification [66][67] for taxonomic and non-taxonomic relation discovery on very large datasets from the Web. The relative redundancy of Web data has allowed this group of techniques that rely on repetitions and regularities to be revived and flourish.
- (Semi)-structured Web data, such as Wikipedia [68] and Freebase [41], have become a necessary part of emerging work for relations discovery.
- Efforts are not being towards the development of new ontology learning tools, but instead towards the improvement of existing ones: increasing in automation, precision, recall and F-measure.

We have also identified the following open issues:

- The fully automatic learning of ontologies may not be possible, considering that an ontology is, after all, a shared conceptualization of a domain.
- The results for discovery of relations between concepts is less than satisfactory.
- The axiom learning from text is currently in the early stages of development.
- There is a lack of reusable services for ontology learning. Many proposed ontology learning methods and approaches highly depend on their specific environment consisting of language, domain, application and input.
- A common evaluation platform for ontologies is currently absent, but is needed.

VI. CONCLUSION AND FUTURE CHALLENGES

This work presented a survey of ontology learning from text. For this intent, we have identified the ontology learning tasks, and introduced, the most used techniques to perform each task. Further, we have provided a comparison table of ontology learning systems, a brief overview of ontology evaluation, and summarized the current trends and open problems in this field. In addition to these problems, the growing use of Web data will introduce new challenges. Firstly, research efforts increasingly be dedicated to creating new, or adapting existing techniques to work with the noise, richness, and diversity of Web data. Secondly, the amount of Web data, which is growing exponentially, will be a significant challenge which merits further attention in the future. Questions of efficiency and robustness in processing data will be at the forefront of this challenge. Thirdly, as more communities of different cultural and linguistic backgrounds contribute to the Web, the availability of textual resources required for multilingual ontology learning will improve. Lastly, as the availability of ontologies increases, ontology alignment will become more pertinent.

REFERENCES

[1] P. Cimiano, J. Volker, and R. Studer, "Ontologies on demand? - a description of the state-of-the-art, applications, challenges and trends for ontology learning from text", Information, Wissenschaft und Praxis, pp. 315-320, 2006.

[2] B. Omelayenko, "Learning of ontologies for the Web: the analysis of existent approaches", In: Proceedings of the International Workshop on Web Dynamics, pp. 16-25, 2001.

[3] V. Novacek, "Ontology learning". Master's thesis, Faculty of Informatics, Masaryk University, Czech Republic, is.muni.cz, 2006.

[4] T. Gruber, "Toward principles for the design of ontologies used for knowledge sharing", International Journal of Human-Computer Studies, pp. 907-928, 1995.

[5] A. Maedche and S. Staab, "Ontology Learning for the Semantic Web", Intelligent Systems, IEEE, pp.72-79 , 2002.

[6] L. Drumond, R. Girardi, "A Survey of Ontology Learning Procedures", Proceedings of the 3rd Workshop on Ontologies and their Applications, vol. 427 of CEUR Workshop Proceedings, Salvador, Bahia, Brazil, 2008.

[7] D. Benz, "Collaborative ontology learning", Master's thesis, University of Freiburg, 2007.

[8] V. Kashyap, "Design and creation of ontologies for environmental information retrieval", Proceedings of the 12th Workshop on Knowledge Acquisition, Modeling and Management (KAW), Banff, Alberta, Canada ,1999.

[9] G. Miller, "Wordnet: a lexical database for english", Commun, ACM 38(11), pp.39-41, 1995.

[10] Wiktionary, accessible from en.wiktionary.org.

[11] M. Rogger and S .Thaler, "Ontology Learning", Seminar paper, Applied Ontology Engineering, Leopold–Franzens–University Innsbruck, 2010.

[12] A. B. Bouiadjra and S. M. Benslimane, "FOEval: Full Ontology Evaluation, Model and Perspectives", In Proceedings of the 7th International Conference on Natural Language Processing and Knowledge Engineering, pp. 464-468, IEEE, Nov. 2011.

[13] P. Cimiano, "Ontology Learning and Population from Text", ISBN: 978-0- 387-30632-2, Springer, 2006.

[14] D. Borigault, C. Jacquemin, and M.-C. L'Homme, editors, "Recent Advances in Computational Terminology", Natural language processing series, vol. 2, pp. 328-332 John Benjamins Publishing Company, 2001.

[15] K. Frantzi and S .Ananiadou, "The c-value / nc-value domain independent method for multiword term extraction", Journal of Natural Language Processing, pp. 145-179, 1999.

[16] P. Pantel and D. Lin, "A statistical corpus-based term extractor", In E. Stroulia and S. Matwin, editors, AI 2001, Lecture Notes in Artificial Intellingence, pp. 36-46, Springer Verlag, 2001.

[17] G. Salton and C. Buckley, "Term-weighting approaches in automatic text retrieval Information Processing & Management 24(5), pp. 515–523, 1988.

[18] G. Miller, R. Beckwith, C. Fellbaum , D. Gross , and K. J. Miller, "Introduction to WordNet: An On-line Lexical Database", International Journal of Lexicography 3, pp. 235-244, Dec. 1990.

[19] D. Bourigault and C. Jacquemin,"Term extraction+ term clustering: An integrated platform for computer-aided terminology", In Proceedings of the ninth conference on European chapter of the Association for Computational Linguistics, pp. 15-22, 1999.

[20] D. Faure and C. Nedellec, "Knowledge acquisition of predicate argument structures from technical texts using machine learning: The system ASIUM". Knowledge Acquisition, Modeling and Management, pp. 329-334, 1999.

[21] A. Maedche and S. Staab, "The text-to-onto ontology learning environment", In Software Demonstration at ICCS-2000-Eight International Conference on Conceptual Structures, Aug., 2000.

[22] E. Drymonas, K. Zervanou, and E. Petrakis, "Unsupervised ontology acquisition from plain texts: The OntoGain system", Natural Language Processing and Information Systems, pp. 277-287, 2010.

[23] P. Buitelaar, P. Cimiano, and B. Magnini, "Ontology Learning from Text: An Overview", Ontology Learning from Text: Methods, Evaluation and Applications, IOS Press, 2005.

[24] D. Hindle, "Noun Classification from Predicate-Argument Structures", In Proceedings of the Annual Meeting of the Association for Computational Linguistic, pp. 268-275, 1990.

[25] D. Lin and P. Pantel, "Induction of Semantic Classes from Natural Language Text", In Proceedings of ACM SIGKDD Conference on Knowledge Discovery and Data Mining, pp. 317-322, 2001.

[26] D. Lin and P. Pantel, "Concept Discovery from Text", In Proceedings of the International Conference on Computational Linguistics (COLING), pp. 577-583, 2002.

[27] M. Reinberger and P. Spyns, "Unsupervised Text Mining for the Learning of DOGMA-inspired Ontologies", Ontology Learning from Text: Methods, Evaluation and Applications, IOS Press, 2005.

[28] R. Evans, "A Framework for Named Entity Recognition in the Open Domain", In Proceedings of the Recent Advances in Natural Language Processing (RANLP-2003), pp. 137-144, 2003.

[29] O. Etzioni et al., "Web-Scale Information Extraction in KnowItAll (Preliminary Results)", In Proceedings of the 13th World Wide Web Conference (WWW), pp. 100-109, 2004.

[30] M. A. Hearst, "Automatic acquisition of hyponyms from large text corpora", In Proceedings of the 14th conference on Computational linguistics, vol. 2, pp. 539-545, Association for Computational Linguistic, 1992.

[31] Z. Harris, Mathematical Structures of Language, John Wiley & Sons, 1968.

[32] M. Sanderson and B. Croft, "Deriving concept hierarchies from text", In Research and Development in Information Retrieval, pp. 206-213. 1999.

[33] T. Rindflesch, L. Tanabe, J. Weinstein, and L. Hunter. Edgar, "Extraction of drugs, genes, and relations from biomedical literature", In Pacific Symposium on Biocomputing, 2000.

[34] J. Pustejovsky, J. Castano, J. Zhang, B. Cochran, and M. Kotecki, "Robust relational parsing over biomedical literature: Extracting inhibit relations", In Pacific Symposium on Biocomputing, 2002.

[35] S. Vintar, L. Todorovski, D. Sonntag, and P. Buitelaar, "Evaluating context features for medical relation mining", In ECML/PKDD Workshop on Data Mining and Text Mining for Bioinformatics, 2003.

[36] A. Maedche and S. Staab, "Discovering conceptual relations from text", In W. Horn, editor, Proceedings of the 14th European Conference on Artificial Intellignece (ECAI'2000), 2000.

[37] D. Lin and P. Pantel, "DIRT - Discovery of Inference Rules from Text", In Proceedings of the ACM SIGKDD Conference on Knowledge Discovery and Data Mining, pp. 323-328, 2001.

[38] D. Lin and P. Pantel, "Induction of Semantic Classes from Natural Language Text", In Proceedings of ACM SIGKDD Conference on Knowledge Discovery and Data Mining, pp. 317-322, 2001.

[39] I. Dagan, O. Glickman, and B. Magnini, "The PASCAL Recognising Textual Entailment Challenge". Lecture Notes in Computer Science, vol. 3944, pp.177-190, Jan. 2006.

[40] D. Faure and C. Nedellec, "Knowledge acquisition of predicate argument structures from technical texts using machine learning: The system ASIUM". Knowledge Acquisition, Modeling and Management, pp. 329-334, 1999.

[41] K. Xu, S. Reddy, Y. Feng, S. Huang, and D. Zhao, "Question Answering on Freebase via Relation Extraction and Textual Evidence", arXiv.org, 2016.

[42] U. Hahn, M. Romacker, and S. Schulz, "MedSynDiKATe--design considerations for an ontologybased medical text understanding system", In Proceedings of the AMIA Symposium, pp. 330-334, American Medical Informatics Association, 2000.

[43] R. Navigli and P. Velardi, "Learning Domain Ontologies from Document Warehouses and Dedicated Websites", Computational Linguistics, 30(2), MIT Press, pp. 151-179, 2004.

[44] X. Jiang and A. H. Tan, "CRCTOL: A semantic- based domain ontology learning system", Journal of the American Society for Information Science and Technology, 61(1), pp. 150-168, 2009.

[45] K. Dellschaft and S. Staab, "Strategies for the evaluation of ontology learning", In Ontology Learning and Population: Bridging the Gap between Text and Knowledge, P. Buitelaar and P. Cimiano, Eds. IOS Press, pp. 253-273, 2008, Amsterdam.

[46] R. Porzel and R. Malaka, "A task-based approach for ontology evaluation", In Proceedings of the 16th European Conference on Artificial Intelligence, Valencia, Spain, Citeseer, 2004.

[47] W. Wong, W. Liu, and M. Bennamoun, "Ontology Learning from Text: A Look Back and into the Future", Article in ACM Computing Surveys, Article 20, Jan. 2011.

[48] Y. Kalfoglou, "Evaluating ontologies during deployment in applications, position statement", OntoWeb 2 meeting, Amsterdam, Dec. 2002.

[49] A. Maedche and S. Staab, "Measuring similarity between ontologies". In Proceedings of the European Conference on Knowledge Acquisition and Management (EKAW), pp. 251-263, 2002.

[50] M. Sabou, C. Wroe, C. Goble and G. Mishne, "Learning domain ontologies for Web service descriptions: An experiment in bioinformatics", In Proceedings of the 14th International Conference on the World Wide Web, pp. 190-198, 2005.

[51] K. Dellschaft and S. Staab, "On how to perform a gold standard based evaluation of ontology learning", In Proceedings of the 5th International Semantic Web Conference (ISWC), pp. 228-241, 2006.

[52] L. Ding et al., "Swoogle: A Search and Metadata Engine for the Semantic Web". In Proceedings of the 13th CIKM, pp. 652-659, 2004.

[53] C. Patel, K. Supekar, Y. Lee, and E. K. Park. OntoKhoj, "A Semantic Web Portal for Ontology Searching, Ranking and Classification", In Proceeding of the Workshop On Web Information And Data Management, pp. 58-61, ACM, 2003.

[54] S. Tartir, I. B. Arpinar, M. Moore, A. P. Sheth, and B. Aleman-Meza, "OntoQA Metric-Based Ontology Quality Analysis", IEEE Workshop on Knowledge Acquisition from Distributed, Autonomous, Semantically Heterogeneous Data and Knowledge Sources, Houston, TX, USA, 2005.

[55] V. Cross and A. Pal, "OntoCAT: An Ontology Consumer Analysis Tool and Its Use on Product Services Categorization Standards", In Proceedings of the First International Workshop on Applications and Business Aspects of the Semantic Web, pp. 44-58, 2006.

[56] M. Jones and H. Alani, "Content-based ontology ranking", In Proceedings of the 9th International Protege Conference, pp. 92-96, 2006.

[57] Y. Wei and J. Chen, "Ranking Ontology based on Structure Analysis", Second International Symposium on Knowledge Acquisition and Modeling IEEE, pp. 119-122, 2009.

[58] A. Zouaq, D. Gasevic, and M. Hatala, "Towards open ontology learning and filtering", Information Systems, vol. 36, no.7, pp. 1064–1081, 2011.

[59] K. Arabshian, P. Danielsen and S. Afroz, "LexOnt: A Semi-Automatic Ontology Creation Tool for Programmable Web", In : AAAI Spring Symposium: Intelligent Web Services Meet Social Computing, pp. 2-8, 2012.

[60] M. Poveda Villalon and MC. Suárez-Figueroa, "OOPS!–OntOlogy Pitfalls Scanner!", oa.upm.es, 2012.

[61] H. Hlomani and D .Stacey, "Approaches, methods, metrics, measures, and subjectivity in ontology evaluation: A survey", Semantic Web Journal, pp. 1-11, 2014.

[62] J. Raad and C. Cruz, "A Survey on Ontology Evaluation Methods", Proceedings of the International Conference on Knowledge Engineering and Ontology Development, pp. 179-186, Nov 2015.

[63] F. Sun, J. Guo, Y. Lan, J. Xu, and X. Cheng, "Learning Word Representations by Jointly Modeling Syntagmatic and Paradigmatic Relations", Proceedings of the 53rd Annual Meeting of the Association for Computational Linguistics, pp. 136-145, 2015.

[64] S. Faralli and S. P. Ponzetto, "DWS at the 2016 Open Knowledge Extraction Challenge: A Hearst-Like Pattern-Based Approach to Hypernym Extraction and Class Induction", Springer: Communications in Computer and Information Science, vol. 641, pp. 48-60, 2016.

[65] J. Gao and S. Mazumda, "Exploiting Linked Open Data to Uncover Entity Types", Springer: Communications in Computer and Information Science, vol. 548, pp. 51-62, 2016.

[66] S. Consoli, D. Reforgiato Recupero, "Using FRED for Named Entity Resolution, Linking and Typing for Knowledge Base Population", Springer: Communications in Computer and Information Science, vol. 548, pp. 40-50, 2016.

[67] T. Kliegr and O. Zamazal, "LHD 2.0: A text mining approach to typing entities in knowledge graphs", Web Semantics: Science, Services and Agents on the World Wide Web, 2016.

[68] P. Arnold and E .Rahm, "Automatic extraction of semantic relations from wikipedia", International Journal on Artificial Intelligence Tools vol. 24, No. 2 , 2015.

[69] S. Landes, C. Leacock and R.I. Tengi, "Building Semantic Concordances", In Christiane Fellbaum (editor), WordNet: an Electronic Lexical Database, pp. 199– 216, MIT Press, Cambridge,1999.

[70] PubMed, accessible from pubmedcentral.nih.gov.

Towards an Automated System for Music Event Detection

Jian Xi*†, Michael Spranger†, Hanna Siewerts† and Dirk Labudde†‡

†University of Applied Sciences Mittweida
Forensic Science Investigation Lab (FoSIL), Germany
Email: {xi, spranger, siewerts}@hs-mittweida.de
‡Fraunhofer
Cyber Security
Darmstadt, Germany
Email: labudde@hs-mittweida.de

***Abstract*—Announcements of events are regularly spread using the Internet, e.g., via online newspapers or social media. Often, these events involve playing music publicly that is protected by international copyright laws. Authorities entrusted with the protection of the artists' interests have to find unregistered music events in order to fully exercise their duty. As a requirement, they need to find texts in the Internet that are related to such events like announcements or reports. However, event detection is a challenging task in the field of Text Mining due to the enormous variety of information that needs to be considered and the large amount of data that needs to be processed. Because no benchmark data is available for the domain of music event detection, in this paper a gold standard dataset is presented and made publicly available for further development and improvement. Subsequently, a process chain for the detection of music events incorporating external knowledge is proposed. Finally, the performance of three classification models is compared using various feature sets and two different datasets. The best performances reach an F_1-measure of 0.94 and 0.946 for the classification of music and music event relevance, respectively.**

Keywords–Event Detection; Text Classification; Categorization; Named Entity Recognition.

I. Introduction

At public events, often, legally protected media, such as music, movies and books are made available to the public. Authorities or private institutions are entrusted with the interests of the artists. This includes transferring them the money collected from registered events. One of the largest private institutions in Germany is the Gesellschaft für musikalische Aufführungs- und mechanische Vervielfältigungsrechte (GEMA, English: Society for musical performing and mechanical reproduction rights) representing the rights of about 2 Million artists all over the world and with a total revenue of 1 Billion Euros a year [1]. However, if event organizers do not register an event, they will cause a loss for the holder of the rights. So far, finding unregistered events after they have taken place is very difficult and is a process mostly done manually.

Nowadays, the information that an event is taking place is often spread using online newspapers, Facebook, Twitter as well as websites. Additionally, after an event has taken place it is often discussed using the same means of communication. Spreading the information this way is often the first choice, as many people can be reached in a short amount of time. Hence, analyzing these textual data makes it possible to automatically find the information needed to uphold the artists' rights. Text Mining, also referred to as Text Analysis, focuses on the analysis of texts in order to receive high level information and latent patterns. For example, it plays an important role in decision making in Business Intelligence, where it can simplify the decision making process by extraction the most valuable information from texts [2]. Event detection is a specific Text Mining problem in which texts are analyzed in order to mine a set of texts that have a semantic link or share conceptual patterns. More generally, it can be seen as a classification problem [3]. Consequently, event detection can be used to find indications of past or future events [4] [5].

This paper addresses music event detection. The goal is to find an appropriate way to detect public music events, which are not officially registered and, therefore, violate copyrights. The amount of data that needs to be taken into account is huge and the data can only be effectively analyzed using machine learning techniques and methods applied in automatized text classification [6].

This paper is organized as follows: In Section II, some related work is briefly reviewed. Sections III and IV describe difficulties in the current domain and the proposed concept. Next to a baseline based on a Naïve Bayes classifier, a Support Vector Machine (SVM), and a Multi-layer Perceptron (MLP) preliminary results will be discussed in Section V. Finally, Section VI gives a short conclusion and discusses future work.

II. Related Work

Basically, event detection is a special mining problem. The aim is to discover new or track previously identified events. In the past years, several different approaches have been developed for closed and open domains. For the former manually designed keyword lists can be used to detect specific events in texts [7]. Those keyword lists work effectively, yet need expert knowledge to define the event-specific keywords. Furthermore, keyword lists are limiting the search framework, which is why they will not work for open domains and can only be used as an additional resource for more complex event types, as is the case with the detection of music events. Another example for the detection of events within a specific field is presented by [8] and [9], both working on the detection of economic events that might influence the market, such as mergers. For open domains, [5] proposed a method using machine learning techniques, like clustering and Named Entity

Recognition (NER) combined with an ontology (DBpedia) in order to classify Tweets into eight predefined event categories.

Similar to event extraction, the recognition of events might also be categorized as data-driven or knowledge-driven event recognition. In [8] and [9] Data-driven approaches were used, both taking mentions of real-world occurrences into account in order to classify their texts into different types of economic events. However, the data-driven approaches fail to consider semantics. In contrast, knowledge-based approaches focus on mining patterns from data to deliver potential rules representing expert knowledge. Depending on the domain or the context, linguistic, lexicographic as well as human knowledge or a combination of these is applied [10].

Much work has been done concerning event detection using different approaches within different fields. Certainly, some of the proposed methods, such as those presented in [7] and [5], can be applied for the detection of music events and our concept is based on the work by [5]. However, in the domain of music event detection, some difficulties appear. For example, events might be announced only using the name of an artist. Some of these difficulties will be discussed in later sections. Additionally, most studies on music event detection so far worked with audio and not text data. One example for a study on music events working with Twitter data is given in [11]. In their study, they identify musical events mentioned in Twitter in order to create a list including sets of artists and venues. The information can be added to an already existing list , for example, a city event calender [11].

III. Data Preparation

Since the nature of the data is very heterogeneous – different sources like Facebook and newspapers are considered – its analysis has inherent challenges. Below, some of them are discussed in more detail.

A. Data Sources

At the beginning of the study, experts, during their work on manually detecting unregistered music events, independently and arbitrarily preselected more than 1000 music event relevant and irrelevant texts from Facebook and online newspapers. This dataset was then annotated as presented below and used as a basis for our gold standard.

B. Challenges

Noisy Data: In general, texts from social media are inherently characterized by noise. For example, texts often include web addresses, telephone numbers, dates and other characters like hashtags. Furthermore, the texts posted, for example, on Facebook or Twitter are not well written in terms of their grammar and orthography. The application of standard NLP tools to correct such mistakes may lead to incorrectly written names of musicians. As these names are crucial for this study, important events may not be detected.

Text Length: Due to technical restrictions and their intended usage, texts in social media are often very short. Information is compressed as much as possible, for example, by using emoticons or abbreviations or by completely leaving out words. Therefore, the application of standard text analysis methods is often difficult, especially, if the method relies on syntactically correct structures. Considering the following text from Facebook, the application of standard Named Entity Recognition methods fails, because some syntactic features are missing:

"Foo Fighters Eintritt 19. in Hamburg"

Latent Information: Taking the example from above, the crucial information that needs to be found is – even if the text is already classified as an event – that Foo Fighters is a band name and, therefore, the text announces a music event. Typically, such information is extracted by applying methods from the field of NER as discussed in [12]. Traditionally, NER is a subtask in the field of information extraction that focuses on locating structured information in a text and assigning it to predefined categories such as names of persons, organizations and locations. However, distinguishing normal persons from singers or normal organizations from bands is challenging and presents one of the biggest problems in the selection of appropriate features as no prior information is available that indicates whether what the NER model identified is really music-related. This can be changed by adding additional information in the gazetter. This means, before the classification it is already known that, f. e., Johann Sebastian Bach is a musician. However, a much more challenging task is the identification of entities in a text such as musicians that are unknown, for example, a new band or DJ. Unfortunately, texts including these entities appear more often than texts announcing events with known entities.

Dynamic Entities: Information is always dynamic and changes in meaning depending on the time of production. The latent new NER-entities (e.g. musicians, bands or groups) change over the time. An example would be the singer and songwriter Ed Sheeran. Before he became a known musician, he would need to have been labeled as a normal person. However, now he needs to be labeled as a musician. This means, which named entities are relevant changes depending on the point of time a text was written. This triggers the requirement to simultaneously update the knowledge base of our system.

C. Gold Standard

Because there are no suitable training data available, it was necessary to create a gold standard as a basis for the training and evaluation of various classification models. As was mentioned above, texts were collected arbitrarily, including 21 texts from online newspapers and 1,097 texts from Facebook. These were manually annotated as music related or music unrelated as well as event related or event unrelated. Both decisions were made independently of each other. Due to text-inherent vagueness, the data was independently labeled by 35 people. In order to ensure the quality of the labeled data, each person was only allowed to work for 2 hours a day.

The final decision regarding what category a text belongs to was made by using a majority criterion. This criterion requires a minimum number of people to agree on a decision in order to provide a confident classification. If the minimum number of agreements was not achieved for a given text, the text was considered ambiguous and removed from the corpus. The minimum number of agreements was derived from a binomial test under the null hypothesis that each decision individually made by every study participant is conducted at random. This hypothesis thus states that $p^+ = p^- = 0.5$, where p^+ and p^- are the decision probabilities. With respect to the null hypothesis, for every number of agreements d a probability $P(d|p^+)$ can be derived from the corresponding binomial distribution. The minimum number of agreements d_{crit} is equal to d, where the null hypothesis can be rejected according to $P(d \geq d_{crit}|p^+) < \alpha$. Here, α corresponds to the Bonferroni-corrected significance level of $0.05/n$, with n being the number of considered texts. In this study, the minimum number of agreements d_{crit} was 29 for the text corpus.

As a result, the corpus consists of 19 newspaper texts and 867 Facebook texts. 335 out of the 867 Facebook texts and 14 out of the 19 newspaper texts are music relevant. Table I provides some descriptive statistics. When music event classification is considered, the number of texts that meet the Bonferroni constraint drops to 505, whereas 251 Facebook texts and 9 online newspaper texts are music event relevant. Table II provides the descriptive statistics for the music event related data. In summary, at the end, two datasets were created: one for music relevance, including 886 texts and one for music event relevance with 505 texts.

TABLE I. STATISTICS OF THE DATA REGARDING MUSIC DETECTION.

	# texts	$\#_{tot}$ *words*	$\#_{avg}$ *words*	shortest	longest
newspaper	19	2071	109	14	387
Facebook	867	85,965	99.1	1	1,238
total	886	87,965	99.3	1	1,238

TABLE II. STATISTICS OF THE DATA REGARDING MUSIC EVENT DETECTION.

	# texts	$\#_{tot}$ *words*	$\#_{avg}$ *words*	shortest	longest
newspaper	13	1,077	82.85	14	277
Facebook	492	59,440	120.81	1	1,238
total	505	60,517	119.84	1	1,238

In order to describe the data in the domain of music events, we defined an XML-schema, with which our raw data can be concisely structured in order to serve as a gold standard to train and test models in this field. Even though this work is focused on music event detection, the schema is constructed to contain various types of event data, such as music, theater, or readings. It includes, beside others, the following information:

- raw text
- source (e. g., Facebook)
- event-related ($\{0, 1\}$ and certainty)
- event-type-related ($\{0, 1\}$ and certainty)
- event location
- event-date
- persons
- different types of roles (e. g., musician, actor)
- different types of events (e. g., music, theater)

It needs to be emphasized that the relation between any text and a specific category is described twice: binary and with a numeric value. The binary description refers to the classification and thus serves as a ground truth, whereas the numeric value represents the degree of certainty. With this gold standard the following areas may be addressed:

- classification of texts regarding different event-types
- recognition of event-related entities, i. e., roles of persons, organizations and locations

Named entities are considered because they provide strong features for the classification, as was shown in [13] and [14]. For example, if the name Eric Clapton, an English singer and songwriter, appears in a text, this is a strong indication that the current text is music related. Since classic NER mostly concentrates on distinguishing between persons, locations, and organizations, a more detailed categorization including some kind of prior knowledge is needed. The entire dataset was annotated and curated manually according to the schema described so far.

IV. PROPOSED CONCEPT

The task of detecting texts concerning music events is a typical categorization task. Categorization, as a special case of classification, attempts to categorize a text into a predefined set of conceptual categories using machine learning techniques. Formally, let $T = t_1, ..., t_m$ be a set of texts to be categorized, and $C = c_1, ..., c_n$ a set of categories, then the task of categorization can be described as surjective mapping $f : T \rightarrow C$, where $f(t) = c \in C$ yields the correct category for $t \in T$. In the field of music event detection, texts need to be assigned to one out of two main classes: related to a music event or not. Texts of the former class can be further categorized into different event types, such as public concerts. This might be of great importance as some music, e. g., religious music or classical music concerts, are license free or public music resources.

Currently, institutions responsible for the enforcement of exploitation rights have to detect unannounced music events predominantly manually and with the help of search engines. This leads to various problems. Firstly, the manual search is very inefficient on large-scale data. Secondly, the manual checking process is error-prone and differs depending on the person who judges the data. Furthermore, the current process chain can hardly be deployed in an online mode due to its semi-automated nature.

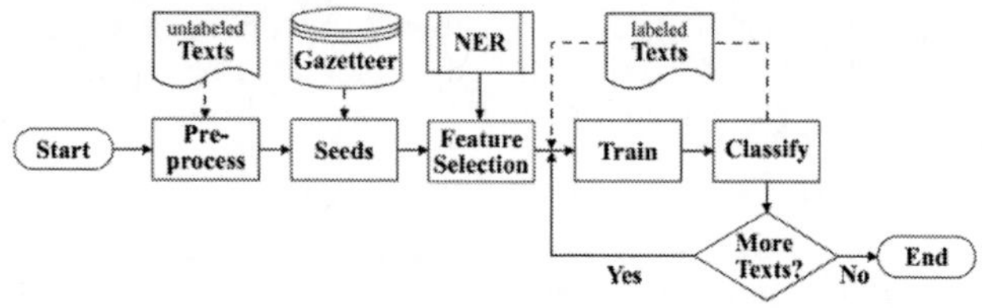

Figure 1. The proposed workflow of music event detection.

To overcome these limitations, a semi-supervised process-chain using a bootstrapping approach, as depicted in Figure 1, is proposed. The advantage of the chosen approach is that the training can start with very few but highly descriptive examples in order to create a first restrictive classifier which will be further improved in upcoming iterations until all texts are classified or no further improvement is possible. Next, each step is discussed in more detail.

A. Preprocessing

As mentioned in Section III-B, the texts we worked on mostly come from the Internet. Such texts often contain typing errors and are often written in informal language, including dialect. This leads to even noisier data than usual in textual texts. Besides common shallow text preprocessing, including stopword and punctuation removal as well as stemming or lemmatizing, there is a strong need for additional language information. This information can be provided in the form of a knowledge base curated by experts. For instance, preselected terms, such as party or live music, can be used to build the gazetteer. Additional useful information might be venues of interest, such as clubs or cafés, where music events often take place. In short, information directly related to music events can be used as a basis of knowledge. This knowledge base can be a simple gazetteer, as is the case in our study, or can incorporate more complex structures, as in [15].

B. Collecting Seed Texts

The most crucial task in bootstrapping is finding seed texts which represent the concept of the classes as well as possible. The usage of some kind of highly descriptive key words or phrases collected from experts in this field is one possible way to find seed texts in a highly accurate, but, nevertheless, very restrictive way. It can be combined with the aforementioned gazetteer.

C. Feature Selection

The next step is the selection of appropriate features to represent the text data. Feature selection is always a critical step in text classification tasks. On the one hand, well selected features are necessary to achieve highly accurate results. On the other hand, they help reduce the feature space and, as a consequence, minimize the time complexity [16]. Traditional frequency-based features, such as Term Frequency (TF), Term Frequency-Inverse Document Frequency (TF-IDF), etc. [6], might not be appropriate in music event detection for two reasons. Firstly, the data often origins from different sources, thus, a term occurring in the training data might not be in new unseen data. Secondly, social media data grows rapidly. Even for a collection with modest size, the TF/TF-IDF matrix will probably be huge. To reduce the dimension of such matrices, the low-rank approximation can be used [17]. However, this approach has a high computational cost.

As was shown in [12]–[14], named entities might be a useful feature for text classification tasks. In a first step, named entities are identified using any NER method, as discussed in [12]. However, as was already discussed in Section III-B, the named entities detected in this way are not specific enough. Hence, domain-specific knowledge resources like MusicBrainz, an open music encyclopedia, and DBpedia can serve as a music database for distinguishing recognized entities further, in order to assign appropriate roles to them, for example, `musician` to a person. The richer this knowledge base, the more accurate is the classification. Hence, the database needs to be maintained in terms of a feedback loop while the model is running. The entire process of music event related Named Entity Recognition is shown in Figure 2. The influence of using NER with a knowledge base is clearly shown in Section V-B.

D. Training and Classification

The final step is to train a first classifier using the seed texts and to try to assign categories to the other texts. This step is repeated until no improvement of the classifier can be achieved or no remaining texts are left.

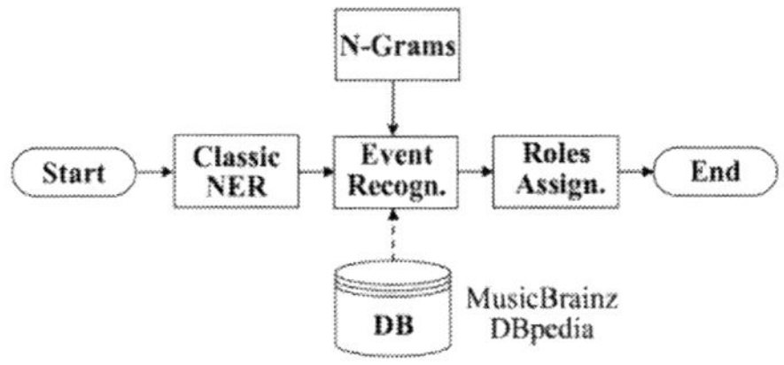

Figure 2. The proposed workflow of detecting music related named entities.

E. System Complexity

In the following section, the system complexity shall be briefly described on the basis of time and space.

Time Complexity: The time complexity of the system, without considering the training and classification process, can be described as shown in Equation 1,

$$\begin{aligned} T(n) &= T_{pre} + T_{gazetteer} + T_{seeds} + T_{ner} + T_{fea_sel} \\ &= O(2^p) + 2O(1) + 3\Theta(lp) + O(L|S|^3) + O(l) \end{aligned} \tag{1}$$

where L is the number of samples and $|S|$ the number of labels in the NER process as well as l the length of the string and p the length of the search pattern in the string.

Space Complexity: Similarly, the space complexity can be measured without considering the training and classification process as shown in Equation 2,

$$\begin{aligned} T(n) &= T_{pre} + T_{gazetteer} + T_{seeds} + T_{ner} + T_{fea_sel} \\ &= O(2^p) + O(g) + \Theta(lp) + O(s+l) + 2\Theta(lp) \\ &\quad + O(r) + O(f) \end{aligned} \tag{2}$$

where g is the size of the gazetteer, r the number of roles, s the size of the trained NER-model and f the number of features. After analyzing the time and space complexity, it can be shown that the system requires intensive resources in preprocessing and in identifying named entities with respect to time and space complexity. Thus, the performance of our system, regarding time and space complexity, depends on the methods that are used in these two setups.

V. Experimental Evaluation

To create first baseline results, the labeled data (see Section III-C) were categorized using three different types of supervised machine learning methods: Naïve Bayes, SVM, and MLP. The categorization was done once with each dataset. Firstly, the dataset with 886 texts was used and categorized as music relevant or not. However, as the ultimate goal is a system for the detection of music events and not just music, secondly, the dataset with only 505 texts was categorized as music event relevant or not.

A. Setup

In this study, only two sources of texts concerning music events are considered: Facebook as well as daily and weekly online newspapers. The raw data were preprocessed as described in Section IV-A. Furthermore, all numbers, for example, telephone numbers and dates, were removed and, therefore, not considered in the categorization. For comparison, two different datasets for each dataset were created. The first dataset contains word tokens that were processed with the Porter stemmer [18], whereas for the second dataset the algorithm proposed in [19] was used. For the detection of named entities a Conditional Random Field approach was applied, as proposed by [20]. As was mentioned in Section IV-C, MusicBrainz und DBpedia were used to assign roles to named entities and were combined in order to increase the number of matches.

In this study, the following four representations of the texts incorporating different features were compared:

- bag of words (BoW) (multinomial BoW),
- TF-IDF of the BoW,
- multinomial BoW and music event related named entities (BoW+NE), and
- TF-IDF of BoW+NE.

In case of named entities only their type (role) was considered as a feature rather than the entity itself, e. g., song writer or musician were taken as a feature instead of Eric Clapton. Moreover, it was only possible to train the SVM with frequency-based features.

B. Results

The baseline results of music relevance decisions of the gold standard dataset described in Section III-C are given in Table III and the results for the categorization of music event relevance are shown in Table IV.

TABLE III. RESULTS FOR 10-FOLD CROSS VALIDATION USING STEMMING AND THE MUSIC RELEVANCE DATASET.

Model	Feature	Micro P.	Micro R.	F_1
Naïve Bayes	BoW	0.686	**0.983**	0.808
	TF-IDF(BoW)	**0.992**	0.676	0.804
	BoW+NE	0.988	0.746	0.850
	TF-IDF(Bow+NE)	0.989	0.782	0.874
MLP	BoW	0.914	0.883	0.898
	TF-IDF(BoW)	0.909	0.911	0.910
	Bow+NE	0.957	0.897	0.926
	TF-IDF(Bow+NE)	0.942	0.937	**0.940**
SVM	TF-IDF(BoW)	0.971	0.868	0.917
	TF-IDF(Bow+NE)	0.981	0.900	0.939

TABLE IV. RESULTS FOR 10-FOLD CROSS VALIDATION USING STEMMING AND THE MUSIC EVENT RELEVANCE DATASET.

Model	Feature	Micro P.	Micro R.	F_1
Naïve Bayes	BoW	0.903	0.951	0.926
	TF-IDF(BoW)	0.893	0.951	0.921
	BoW+NE	0.920	0.962	0.941
	TF-IDF(Bow+NE)	0.901	**0.966**	0.932
MLP	BoW	0.929	0.901	0.915
	TF-IDF(BoW)	0.904	0.932	0.918
	Bow+NE	**0.957**	0.935	**0.946**
	TF-IDF(Bow+NE)	0.929	0.951	0.940
SVM	TF-IDF(BoW)	0.938	0.920	0.929
	TF-IDF(Bow+NE)	**0.957**	0.920	0.938

The models were evaluated using a 10-fold cross validation and by calculating the harmonic mean (F_1) of the micro-averaged precision and sensitivity. The tables show the results using stemming. The results were compared with those achieved using lemmatization and it was observed that stemming lead to slightly better results. As can be seen in Table III, the best results for the categorization of music relevance, based on the F_1-measure, were achieved using a frequency-based representation of words and named entities (roles) and MLP. In comparison, a combination of BoW and named entities (roles) and an MLP model achieved the best results for the categorization of music event relevance. These results are presented in Table IV. Furthermore, it was found that the best performing model and feature combination (MLP and BOW+NE) failed if the features (word) were in both, the relevant and non-relevant texts, as well as when the texts were very short or not enough strong features were available to the model. The results in both tables show that the classification results of music relevance are clearly improved when the NER features are considered.

VI. CONCLUSION AND FUTURE WORK

In this paper, two gold standard datasets for music event detection were presented and will be made publicly available here [21]. Furthermore, a process chain for the categorization of music event related texts was proposed and a first baseline evaluation conducted. The results show that a frequency-based approach and music specific named entities together with a multi-layer perceptron model performs best for the classification of music relevant texts in comparison to a BoW and named entities representation with an SVM for the classification of music event relevance. The results for both datasets are very similar and show that adding named entities leads to an improvement in the performance.

The datasets used were relatively small, especially the one including music event related texts and shall be extended in the future. Furthermore, future research should also focus on improving the performance, i. e., by considering the Entity Power Coefficient, as shown in [13] [14], or active learning, as described in [22] [23]. Currently, some kind of neural probabilistic language models [24] are tested. Such models provide another way to represent a text by learning a distributed representation of words which enables each training sentence to inform the model about an exponential number of semantically neighboring sentences. Additionally, music events including music that does not fall under any copyright laws need to be distinguished from those events that might include copyright infringements. For this purpose, a more fine-grained categorization to separate different types of events can be realized by applying hierarchical classification methods, such as discussed in [14] [25].

ACKNOWLEDGMENT

The authors would like to thank the deecoob GmbH for acting as experts during the creation of the gold standard and providing data. The project was funded by the German federal ministry for economics and energy.

REFERENCES

[1] GEMA, "Geschäftsbericht mit Transparenzbericht 2017," https://www.gema.de/fileadmin/user_upload/Gema/geschaeftsberichte/GEMA_Geschaeftsbericht2017.pdf, 2018 [retrieved: September, 2018].

[2] F. Carsten, Text Mining als Anwendungsbereich von Business Intelligence. Springer, Berlin, Heidelberg, 2006, pp. 283–304.

[3] Y. Yang, T. Pierce, and J. Carbonell, "A Study of Retrospective and Online Event Detection," in Proceedings of the 21st Annual International ACM SIGIR Conference on Research and Development in Information Retrieval. ACM, 1998, pp. 28–36.

[4] K. Giridhar and A. James, "Text Classification and Named Entities for New Event Detection," in Proceedings of the 27th Annual International ACM SIGIR Conference on Research and Development in Information Retrieval. ACM, 2004, pp. 297–304.

[5] A. Edouard, "Event detection and analysis on short text messages," Ph.D. dissertation, Université Côte D'Azur, 2017, https://hal.inria.fr/tel-01680769/document [retrieved: September, 2018].

[6] M. Ikonomakis, S. Kotsiantis, and V. Tampakas, "Text Classification Using Machine Learning Techniques," WSEAS Transactions on Computers, vol. 4, 2006, pp. 966–974.

[7] T. Sakaki, M. Okazaki, and Y. Matsuo, "Earthquake shakes twitter users: Real-time event detection by social sensors," in Proceedings of the 19th International Conference on World Wide Web. ACM, 2010, pp. 851–860.

[8] E. Lefever and V. Hoste, "A classification-based approach to economic event detection in dutch news text," in Proceedings of the Tenth International Conference on Language Resources and Evaluation. European Language Resources Association (ELRA), 2016, pp. 330–335.

[9] G. Jacobs, E. Lefever, and V. Hoste, "Economic event detection in company-specific news text," in Proceedings of the First Workshop on Economics and Natural Language Processing. Association for Computational Linguistics, 2018, pp. 1–10.

[10] F. Hogenboom, F. Frasincar, U. Kaymak, and F. de Jong, "An overview of event extraction from text," in CEUR Workshop Proceedings, vol. 779, 2011, pp. 48–57.

[11] E. Benson, A. Haghighi, and R. Barzilay, "Event discovery in social media feeds," in Proceedings of the 49th Annual Meeting of the Association for Computational Linguistics: Human Language Technologies - Volume 1, ser. HLT '11. Stroudsburg, PA, USA: Association for Computational Linguistics, 2011, pp. 389–398.

[12] D. Nadeau and S. Sekine, "A survey of named entity recognition and classification," Linguisticae Investigationes, vol. 30, 2007, pp. 3–26.

[13] M. K. Stefan Andelic, "Text classification based on named entities," 2017, pp. 23–28.

[14] Y. Gui, Z. Gao, R. Li, and X. Yang, "Hierarchical text classification for news articles based-on named entities," Advanced Data Mining and Applications, vol. 7713, 2012, pp. 318–329.

[15] M. Spranger and D. Labudde, "Towards Establishing an Expert System for Forensic Text Analysis," International Journal on Advances in Intelligent Systems, vol. 7, no. 1/2, 2014, pp. 247–256.

[16] Y. Yang and J. O. Pedersen, "A comparative study on feature selection in text categorization," in Proceedings of the Fourteenth International Conference on Machine Learning, 1997, pp. 412–420.

[17] G. W. Furnas et al., "Information retrieval using a singular value decomposition model of latent semantic structure," in Proceedings of the 11th Annual International ACM SIGIR Conference on Research and Development in Information Retrieval, ser. SIGIR '88. ACM, 1988, pp. 465–480.

[18] M. F. Porter, "An algorithm for suffix stripping," Program, vol. 14, no. 3, 1980, pp. 130–137.

[19] H. Schmid and H. Schmid, "Improvements in part-of-speech tagging with an application to german," Proceedings of the ACL SIGDAT-Workshop, 1995, pp. 47—50.

[20] J. R. Finkel, T. Grenager, and C. Manning, "Incorporating non-local information into information extraction systems by gibbs sampling," in Proceedings of the 43rd Annual Meeting on Association for Computational Linguistics. ACM, 2005, pp. 363–370.

[21] J. Xi, "Music Classification Gold Standard Datasets," https://github.com/fosil-mw/music_classification_data, 2018 [retrieved: November, 2018].

[22] Q. Yang and S. J. Pan, "A Survey on Transfer Learning," IEEE Transactions on Knowledge Data Engineering, vol. 22, 2009, pp. 1345–1359.

[23] D. K. Xiao Li and C. X. Ling, "Active learning for hierarchical text classification," Tan PN., Chawla S., Ho C.K., Bailey J. (eds) Advances in Knowledge Discovery and Data Mining, vol. 7301, 2012, pp. 14–25.

[24] Y. Bengio, R. Ducharme, P. Vincent, and C. Janvin, "A neural probabilistic language model," Journal of Machine Learning Research, vol. 3, 2003, pp. 1137–1155.

[25] A. McCallum, R. Rosenfeld, T. M. Mitchell, and A. Y. Ng, "Improving text classification by shrinkage in a hierarchy of classes," in Proceedings of the Fifteenth International Conference on Machine Learning, 1997, pp. 359–367.

Italian Domain-specific Thesaurus as a Means of Semantic Control for Cybersecurity Terminology

Claudia Lanza
Department of Computer Engineering, Modelling, Electronics and Systems Engineering (DIMES)
University of Calabria
Arcavacata di Rende, Italy
e-mail: c.lanza@dimes.unical.it

Abstract— **This paper presents an ongoing PhD research project aimed at realizing a tool for semantic control - an Italian thesaurus - that could represent a repository of the Cybersecurity field of knowledge and a means starting from which the representativeness of this domain can be enhanced by increasing the terminological coverage threshold. The paper starts with a description of the methodology followed by the creation of an authoritative corpus. This latter is meant to be the source of the information retrieval for the terms that should be inserted in the Italian controlled vocabulary of Cybersecurity. Afterwards, an overall summary of the semi-automatic terminological extraction will be provided. The paper focuses on the terminological process of mapping the selected terms from the authoritative corpus to the existent standards of Information and Communications Technology Security glossaries and vocabularies by using Python scripts. The paper also focuses on the perspective of how the relationships built in a thesaurus could be migrated to an ontology as a better form of knowledge representation.**

Keywords-Cybersecurity; knowledge representation; information retrieval; ontologies; thesauri.

I. Introduction

The underlying idea of this PhD research project is to develop a model that is meant to guarantee the terminological coverage of a semantic resource, such as a thesaurus, and its representativeness threshold with reference to semantic variation during time. By building an Italian thesaurus related to the Cybersecurity domain, this project relies on the perspective of providing organizations with a complete knowledge representation of the field of study on Information and Communications Technology (ICT) security. The thesaurus can represent a valid support tool for information access, treatment of data and information retrieval tasks in order to improve the security decision making processes. This research project is included in one of the activities carried out in collaboration with the Informatics and Telematics Institute (IIT) [26] – National Research Council (CNR) institute located in Pisa.

This paper analyses the steps needed to construct the thesaurus related to this particular domain beginning with the selection of the sources, which have been taken into consideration in order to have an authoritative corpus from which the information of the domain can be retrieved. The goal of the research project is, therefore, to provide a solid tool in which the information on Cybersecurity could help in reaching as complete a terminological coverage as possible. To reach this latter perspective, the project aims at enhancing the terminological set of data by taking into account not only legislative documents but also social media infrastructures and, doing so, achieves a heterogeneous information repository.

The main intention of the research project is to create an Italian thesaurus on Cybersecurity, currently not existing, that can help organizations to better frame the information on Cybersecurity and provide a terminological means of support that could be useful to broadly understand the domain from a semantic point of view. Even though there are taxonomies and glossaries on Cybersecurity in Italian language, such as, for example [15], a thesaurus can be considered a service that could give a more detailed overview on this domain thanks to the possibility of creating relationships between the terms that are meant to be representative of this area of study. The semantic tangle that comes out by the creation of a thesaurus is a starting point that can facilitate the process of migrating the knowledge organization within it into an ontology system.

The purpose of this paper is threefold: (1) providing an overall presentation of how to build a semantic tool, such as a thesaurus, as a means of semantic control for a specific domain by describing the steps which characterize the corpus creation and the terminological extraction; (2) presenting a model of mapping the existent standards on Cybersecurity to all the head terms contained in the initial corpus through Python scripts in order to evaluate which candidate terms should be chosen to be part of the thesaurus; (3) opening up the perspective of migrating the terms and their relationships of the Italian thesaurus on Cybersecurity in an ontology system.

The paper is structured into five sections. Section II contains a brief presentation of the state of the art consulted for the creation of the Italian thesaurus on Cybersecurity. The studies taken into consideration in Section II specifically refer to strategies able to establish the terminological coverage threshold of a semantic resource. Section III goes deeper into the methodological approach undertaken towards the realization of the semantic means of control on this particular domain. It describes the phases related to the information retrieval, starting with the authoritative set of documents that make up the source corpus. Section IV describes the way in which the terminological extraction has been executed from these texts by using the Text to Knowledge (T2K software). Section V outlines the methods employed to select the head-based terms with a particular overview on a mapping system between the glossary derived from the terminological extraction and the major standards vocabularies on the Cybersecurity domain, i.e., this section ends with a description of a Python script used to automatize the process of aligning the terms contained in the standards and the terms obtained by the terminological extraction. Finally, Section VI concludes the paper with the proposal of converting the semantic structure of the thesaurus into an ontology system by migrating not only the terms, but also the relationships.

II. State of the Art

Many studies on the issue of evaluating the qualitative strength of a thesaurus have been carried out, like [23], which gives practical suggestions on how to create a reliable semantic resource. Other works have focused their attention on the importance of having a group of people with a high expertise in the domain that has to be analysed for the purposes of realizing a semantic tool for information retrieval. For example, [16] deals with the advantage of getting helped by domain experts who can increase the value of a thesaurus especially for what concerns the selection of terms and their relationships. Another study that is worth mentioning for its important description of a way by which corpus representativeness can be measured is [22]. The authors provide statistical formulas to calculate the size threshold of corpora in terms of linguistic coverage of a particular domain of interest. To calculate the ideal situation in which a semantic tool like a thesaurus can continue to be representative with respect to a particular domain, the terminological update within it is an unavoidable aspect to take into account, and [17] addresses this issue in greater detail.

One of the difficulties faced to set up the construction of the Italian controlled vocabulary, that aims at including as much information about Cybersecurity as possible, is that the available Italian sources on this subject seem to be quite few. A list of some Italian resources that have been used to extract information is given in Section III, *Corpus Creation*. The challenge, therefore, is to map the English concepts inside various terminological repositories on the Cybersecurity field to the Italian language and, by doing so, to align the description of these terms with the Italian law systems and ICT shared knowledge. There are many studies which have been carried out to develop reliable terminological sources that could guide the understanding of the Cybersecurity domain and help with the information retrieval on this subject for the creation of the Italian Cybersecurity thesaurus. Among these aforementioned studies, [8] contains one well-defined example of a helpful ontology on this subject displaying various ways of correlating Cybersecurity concepts in a semantic network process. [9] also gives light to some of the most common terms used in Cybersecurity, and [10] collects the terminology referred to the cyber-threats accompanied by the descriptions of all the terms of this repository. The latter has been helpful in placing the relationships inside the Italian thesaurus. Other important repositories that contributed to the population of terms referred to Cybersecurity vulnerabilities and threats or attacks, are the ones collected in the MITRE Corporation systems [13][14].

III. Methodological Approach

The first step of the project is based on the retrieval of the terminological authoritative sources that are going to be the documentary corpus of the domain that has to be analysed. Subsequently, a terminological extraction from the selected documents is carried out through specific programs that are meant to execute text-processing tasks. Next, the paper describes the steps according to which a thesaurus is going to be realized starting from a validation of terms by experts belonging to the domain of interest. With the output given by the terminological extraction, that is the controlled terminological list of terms sorted by the Term Frequency–Inverse Document Frequency (TF/IDF) measurement, a process of selection of the head-based terms begins by mapping the terms of the source corpus with the existent standards of ICT Security. Head-based terms are single terms that appear with highest frequency in the texts and that bring together other terms with which they are frequently accompanied, i.e., if "access" appears accompanied with many other lexical units, thus it will be the head-based term that will help in positioning its qualifiers and other terms with which occurs in the thesaurus.

For a better understanding of the system that has driven towards construction of a semantic means of control on Cybersecurity, the following Unified Modelling Language (UML) activity diagram [11] depicts the steps taken for the realization of the Italian thesaurus on this field of knowledge (Fig. 1).

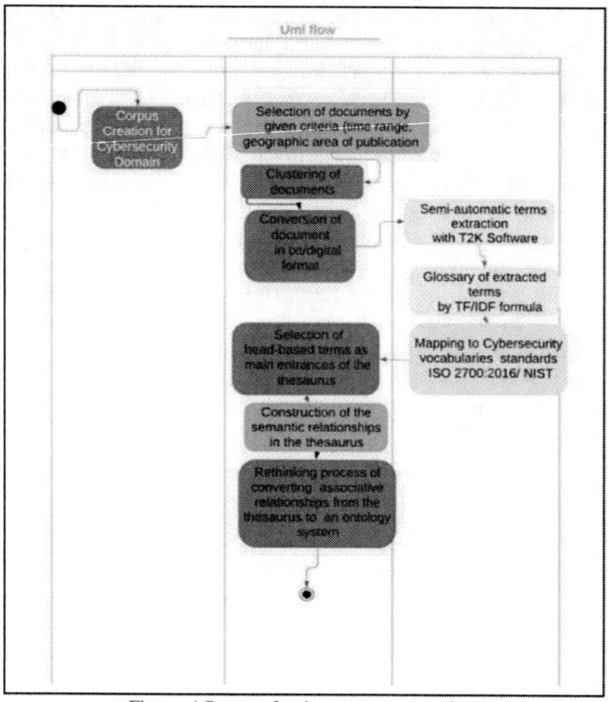

Figure. 1 Process for thesaurus construction.

The first phase of the ongoing project has dealt with the identification, the retrieval and the analysis of the existing Italian authoritative terminological sources referring to the domain of Cybersecurity. The material collected represents the reference context of ICT security and contains, as well, an important dataset both from a quantitative and qualitative point of view.

In terms of the quantitative evaluation of the documents which a corpus is supposed to contain, an established estimate does not exist in the literature. However, it is recommended to have a sizeable set of data that belong to the specific domain of Cybersecurity and consequently have a terminological coverage that could make its representativeness strong enough; a highly reliable dataset should also be present from a qualitative point of view so that the construction of a thesaurus could be as accurate as possible. The sources consulted must be considered authoritative in order for the thesaurus to become a guide that pilots the correct management of the sector-specific language. This process of gathering authoritative sources in order to make the semantic tool wide ranging is based on the principle of the hierarchy of the sources that in law considers three levels: constitutional sources (Constitution, constitutional laws and constitutional revision); legislative sources, also called primary sources (laws, decree law and legislative decree, regional laws) [7]; regulatory laws, also called secondary sources (Government Laws, local authoritative) – books, magazines and specialized articles, field specialized user profiles (experts of Cybersecurity) or social media users. One of the future prospects that will be considered for the development of this proposal is the attention to the social media world, referring to the wisdom of the crowds [2] according to which the implementation of new terms that, over time, become much more common in media jargon, should be considered in detail to understand the necessity of inserting them into the controlled vocabulary.

It goes without saying that this heterogeneity of documents that marks the source corpus from which the information about the domain is going to be studied is a remarkable advantage to reach a higher level of representativeness threshold. To give an example, in the source corpus, various documents deriving from different format and typologies have been taken into consideration, among these:

- Decree Laws;
- Parliamentary legislation;
- Penal/Administrative/Civil Code;
- Rules (GDPR);
- CERT guidelines;
- Government documents;
- Magazines that deal with the domain topics and could give another terminological output to enhance the thesaurus coverage (i.e., “Gnosis”, “Hacker Journal”).
- Glossaries (i.e., “Intelligence Glossary” [15])

Having to do with a domain under development, the hope is to run with the terminological evolution within the corpora so as to test through time the structure of the persistent value of the semantic relationships inside the thesaurus with the emergence of new terms and with the updating of the existing ones.

The constructed corpus will be the starting point from where a thesaurus will be realized and it will be characterized by a flexible set of documents that are going to vary over the years and that will be a very important aspect in order to enhance the terminological coverage level of a given domain of study.

The representativeness of a thesaurus is the key to determine its authoritativeness with respect to certain domains and geographic positioning areas. After completing the construction of the thesaurus structure, reaching what is considered to be the “gold standard” is the first purpose that the research activity aims at. It is unquestionable that this purpose could be reached only after the candidate terms have passed through a validation process by specific field experts. The latter, thanks to their level of authoritativeness in the areas of competence, represents a key step that cannot be avoided to have the approval of terms and of their semantic associations in the systems of knowledge management and organization. The international standards of reference, such as the 25964-1 of 2011 [3] and ISO 2564-2 of 2013 [4] regulations, will be followed: they will provide a standardization of the terms contained in the thesaurus that can guarantee the interoperability between various systems of knowledge management.

IV. TERMINOLOGICAL EXTRACTION

The terminological extraction is carried out once the corpus has been defined by the selection of documents which come from the authoritative legislative sources and informative channels, such as the official magazines that contain information about the domain taken into account.

Before beginning with a semi-automatic processing of the information contained in the source corpus, the digital native documents, downloaded from the websites of the authoritative sources or Web portals, have been converted into txt format, which is the format required by the textual analysis software.

Native paper documents have been firstly scanned and saved as PDF files and have then undergone an optical character recognition process and finally transformed into txt documents.

Among the pieces of software that have been chosen for the terminological extraction, the Text To Knowledge (T2K) [25] tool has been preferred for the purposes of detecting, in further analysis, head terms that can become part of the controlled vocabulary.

T2K is a software developed by the Institute for Computational Linguistics (ILC – CNR) in Pisa (Italy) by a group of computational linguists and it is a powerful Natural Language Processing (NLP) tool that can provide, through semi-automatic text processing tasks, different forms of wordlists which include candidate terms used to populate the thesaurus. T2K allows to extrapolate the most relevant terms of the corpus on Cloud systems or by virtualization techniques, according to variables, such as accuracy – obtained by the algorithm ULISSE [18] – occurrence, frequency and disambiguation.

The first steps of this project have dealt with the lexical configuration in T2K of the desired semantic chains as output from the documents that make up the imported corpus. What has been obtained by the semi-automatic processing of T2K is a glossary of terms that refer to the domain of study which is meant to be used for the semantic analysis of the candidate terms derived from this set of authoritative digital and paper sources. The statistical measurement that characterized the basis of the terminological representation of the candidate terms in the T2K wordlist is the TF/IDF formula. According to this statistical measurement, the lexical units with the highest frequency are considered less important – such as, adverbs, or articles and prepositions, in brief the stopwords – and the output underlines the words that occur in the documents that in general are less frequent.

Only after having set the semantic configuration of the lexical units of the output given by the NLP text processing, T2K provides different ways to visualize the terms that are meant to be part of the controlled vocabulary. One of these, the so-called Broader Term (BT/NT), that corresponds to the ISO [3][4] tag standard, has been selected in order to help with the decision of inserting preferred candidate terms in the thesaurus. For a better understanding of the results of terms from the authoritative corpus, the following figures show the table given by the extraction (Fig. 2), and the knowledge graph derived from the occurrences of these terms with others inside the corpus (Fig 3). Both of these processes have been developed by using the semi-automatic terminological extraction of T2K NLP Tool. The knowledge graph is a representation of terms that are connected together, and this is the way followed for the selection of the most pertinent head-based terms.

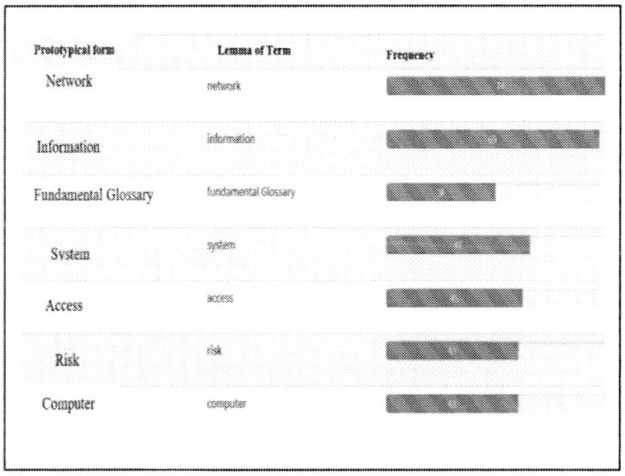

Figure. 2 Example of terms extracted with T2K.

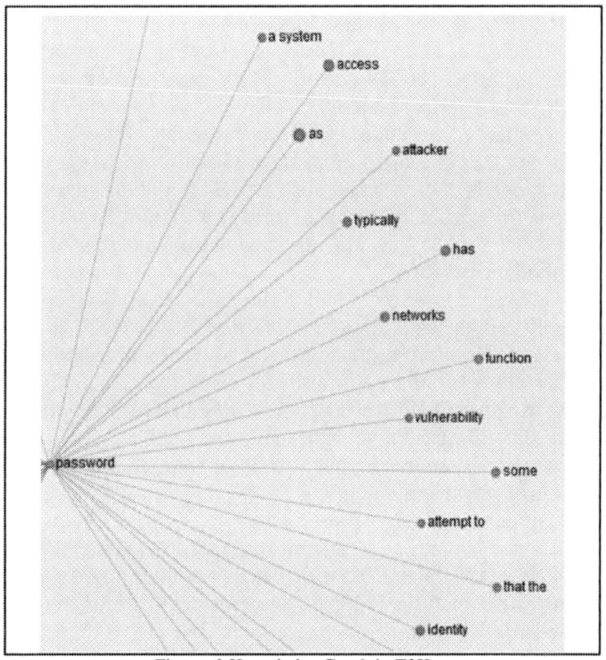

Figure. 3 Knowledge Graph in T2K.

V. HEAD-BASED TERMS

A semantic tool, such as a thesaurus, should represent a reliable source of information that can support the operations of information retrieval and the access to documents related to a specific domain of study. For this reason, the first phase that follows up on the creation of a corpus and the terminological extraction from these authoritative documents is strictly connected to the selection of which candidate terms should be considered as preferred terms that are to be imported in the controlled vocabulary and starting from which the basic relationships proper of a thesaurus can be inserted.

Typically, in a thesaurus, the classical kinds of relationships that characterize the network of connections between terms are of three types, as [1][3][4] better explain:

1. Equivalent relationship characterizes the synonymy or quasi-synonymy between different terms; in a thesaurus there is one term that is going to be considered as the preferred one to which the other kind of relationships can be developed and it is marked by a tag USE, and its synonym, or the other way by which it can be seen in the domain documents, is marked by the tag UF that stands for *Used For*, e.g., VAPT UF Vulnerability Assessment and Penetration Testing;
2. Hierarchical relationship is marked by two tags: BT that stands for *Broader Term* and represents the more general concept with reference to its more specific one which is, on the other hand, marked as NT, i.e., *Narrower Term*, e.g., Cyber Attacks NT Brute force attacks, or Cyber Threats NT Hacker;
3. Associative relationship defined by the standard tag RT that stands for *Related Term*: it represents a concept that is associated to another one, e.g., Hacker RT Cyber criminality, or Spam RT Virus; as [3] stated, "the associative relationship covers associations between pairs of concepts that are not related hierarchically, but are semantically or conceptually associated to such an extent that the link between them needs to be made explicit in the thesaurus, on the grounds that it may suggest additional or alternative terms for use in indexing or retrieval. The relationship is indicated by the tag 'RT' (related term) and it should be applied reciprocally".

In order to make the Italian thesaurus on Cybersecurity a highly representative source, this paper describes a project phase that has covered the retrieval of terms contained in the NIST Glossary of Key Information Security Terms 7298 [5] and in the ISO-IEC 27000/2016 [6] standard. The purpose was that of checking if those terminological assets were present in the source corpus that has created the basis for the terminological extraction.

Since the source corpus is made up of documents written in Italian language, in order to create a semantic tool for Cybersecurity in Italian, which does not currently exist, the contrastive analysis with the glossaries in the aforementioned standards is useful for three main reasons: (1) because mapping the standard terms can prove, by verifying their presence in the source corpus, if the latter, built for the construction of an Italian thesaurus of Cybersecurity, can be conveyed as a reliable resource; (2) because matching them with the BT/NT structure of the terminological controlled list obtained through text processing software operations is a way of detecting which can be the preferred terms in the thesaurus; (3) starting from the scope notes contained in these standards, the network of the relationships that will characterize the thesaurus can comply as much as possible with the domain language usage.

The steps undertaken to analyse the standard terms list with the terms contained in the source corpus are the following:

1. After having downloaded the NIST 7298 [5] and ISO-IEC 27000/2016 [6], they have been semi-manually translated into Italian language in order to better suit the purposes of the project research of creating an Italian resource for Cybersecurity terminology retrieval; the tool that has been employed to proceed with the translation of the terms present in the ICT standards and their definitions, is TRADOS [12]. This service provides a memory repository that can catch all the translations that have been made on a document which can be used whenever, in another document, there is a term that can be translated exactly the same as in previous texts; this is highly useful in order to achieve coherence in the translation process of many texts;
2. The list of terms contained in the aforementioned standards have been assessed by a group of experts who have played an essential role in the validation of the authoritative source terms to start the cross mapping in the source corpus;
3. A Python script has been realized in order to check if all the words present in the standards were also included in the list obtained by the terminological extraction under the hierarchical form BT/NT. This script takes into account the terminological list from the whole corpus and, through a reading of its lines, the content of the file becomes analysable. Subsequently, an automatic generation of an output file text gives a list of all the occurrences (terms contained in the standards that are present in the controlled list) all at once, facilitating a screening process of the mapping system;
4. Once verified the presence or the absence of determined terms that are inserted in the standards taken into consideration, a process of selection among the head-based terms resulted from the extraction with T2K has been started with the help of the domain experts. Collaboration with the domain experts continues in order to face the challenge of deciding which terms can be considered as the best head terms that can connect the others inside the list and the standards;
5. After having chosen which terms could be considered as the preferred entries in the future Italian thesaurus, the process of building the network of the relationships has begun starting from the term definitions in the standards, and that helped in positioning the terms connected with each other in the thesaurus;
6. A draft prototype of an Italian thesaurus for Cybersecurity has been realized equipped with the Scope Notes derived from the definitions in the standards.

VI. CONCLUSION

This paper aimed at presenting an ongoing work based on a PhD research project that refers to the construction of an Italian Cybersecurity thesaurus, whose terminological coverage is going to be semi-automatically enhanced.

The goal set out in this PhD path is that of migrating all the relationships that will be created in the thesaurus into relationships inside a different structure, i.e., an ontology system.

A large number of studies on the possibility of reengineering a thesaurus into an ontology have proved that this conversion is possible through the migration of the typologies of relationships in the basic ones of the ontology. In [24], the authors have developed a methodology able to convert the basic relationships proper of the thesaurus to Web Ontology Language (OWL) language. In [19], for the AGROVOC domain, the study converged on a set of relationships the replacement of those used in a thesaurus making them more specific. Indeed, the objective behind the need of converting the thesaurus into an ontology is based mainly on the principle that the latter provides a deeper knowledge representation.

One of the most evident differences that occur between a thesaurus and an ontology is that the associative relationship in the former, RT, can be clarified by customized form of related connections which can be themselves split in different hierarchical and more specific subclasses of relationships. As [21] demonstrates with their experiment of migrating the MeSH thesaurus with OWL language, one of the limits of a thesaurus is that of providing a flattened base of knowledge in terms of RT connections among terms. Although a thesaurus can be a reliable form of domain-specific information retrieval, and can create a dense net of connections which can generate a cross-reference system able to gather all the terminology in a determined field of study, the associative relationship does not suffice to formalize the conceptual links between terms. For this reason, also [20] offers a wide perspective on this issue with its Hasti project, an ontology is able to detect a more specialized kind of relationship customizing, by Universal Resource Identifier (URI) names, the typology of every one of these relationships that have to be different in order to handle a deeper form of knowledge organization of the domain that has to be represented.

The purpose of the conversion from a thesaurus to an ontology is to make information readable through languages that are proper to the ontologies: Resource Description Framework (RDF), Resource Description Framework Schema (RDFs), OWL. The transposition of the concepts represented through an abstract level by terms into an ontology should work to provide a better semantic representation system of the network of relationships. Thanks to OWL, it is possible to have extra semantic properties, such as the disjunction between two sets, so a complex of concepts can be separately analysed, the functional association of a property to a class and consequently the establishment of unique identifiers; the transitive property between classes useful for the creation of a much more articulate and descriptive semantic network. The efficiency of OWL relies on its formalism of language and in the possibility of applying automatic reasoning systems and developing inference on the described knowledge.

Even converting terms inside the controlled vocabulary into a class, entity and property scheme that belongs to a conceptual ontological modelling, the presence of a group of experts who will validate the associative network obtained by the reconstruction of the thesaurus in an ontology will be necessary.

ACKNOWLEDGMENT

This work has received the support of the [26] at the National Research Council in Pisa, especially by the emerging Cybersecurity group.

REFERENCES

[1] W. Broughton, "Building thesauri", Milan, 2006.

[2] J. Surowiecki, Wisdom of crowds, Anchor Books, 2004.

[3] International Standard ISO 25964-1, "Information and documentation — Thesauri and interoperability with other vocabularies — Part 1: Thesauri for information retrieval", First edition 2011-08-15.

[4] International Standard ISO 25964-2, "Information and documentation — Thesauri and interoperability with other vocabularies — Part 2: Interoperability with other vocabularies", First edition 2013-03-15.

[5] R. Kisserl, NISTIR 7298 Revision 2 "Glossary of Key Information Security Terms" National Institute of Standards and Technology Interagency or Internal Report 7298r2, May 2013.

[6] International Standard ISO/IEC 27000:2016 (E) Information technology – Security techniques – Information security management systems – Overview and vocabulary, Fourth edition 2016-02-05.

[7] V. Crisafulli , "Hierarchy and competence in the constitutional system of law sources" in "Studies in the memory of Guido Zanobini". Milan: Giuffrè, 1965, vol. III, p. 183.; G. Zagrebelsky, The constitutional system of law sources. Turin: EGES 1984, p. 67;

[8] Z. Syed, A. Padia, T. Finin, L. Mathews and A. Joshi, "UCO: Unified Cybersecurity Ontology, AAAI Workshop on Artificial Intelligence for Cyber Security", February 2016.

[9] NICCS National Initiative for Cybersecurity Careers and Studies – Glossary, https://niccs.us-cert.gov/about-niccs/glossary [accessed October 2018] .

[10] Sophos "Threatsaurus The A-Z of Computer and data security threats", https://www.sophos.com/en-us/medialibrary/PDFs/other/sophosthreatsaurusaz.pdf?la=en [accessed September 2018]

[11] Argo Uml, https://argouml.it.uptodown.com/windows [accessed October 2018]

[12] SDL Trados Studio, https://www.sdltrados.com/it/ [accessed October 2018]

[13] "The Common Vulnerabilities and Exposures (CVE) Initiative", MITRE Corporation, https://cve.mitre.org/ [accessed September 2018]

[14] "The Common Attack Pattern Enumeration and Classification (CAPEC) Initiative", MITRE Corporation, https://capec.mitre.org/ [accessed September 2018]

[15] Presidenza del Consiglio dei Ministri – Sistema di informazione per la sicurezza della Repubblica, "Il linguaggio degli Organismi Informativi", Glossario Intelligence, https://www.sicurezzanazionale.gov.it/sisr.nsf/quaderni-di-intelligence/glossario-intelligence.html. [accessed October 2018]

[16] Claire K. Shultz, Wallace L. Schultz, and Richard H. Orr, "Evaluation of Indexing by Group Consensum" (Final Report, Contract No OEC 1-7-070622-3890), Bureau of Research Office of Education, U.S. Department of Health, Education and Welfare, August 30, 1968, 40 pp.

[17] A. Kennedy and S. Szpakowicz, "Evaluation of automatic updates of Roget's Thesaurus" J. Language Modelling, 2014, volume 2, pp.1-49 .

[18] F. Dell'Orletta, G. Venturi, and S. Montemagni, "ULISSE: An Unsupervised Algorithm for Detecting Reliable Dependency Parser", Conference: Proceedings of the Fifteenth Conference on Computational Natural Language Learning, 2011, pp. 115-124.

[19] D. Sorgel et al., "Reeingeenering Thesauri for New Applications: the AGROVOC Example", J. Dig. Inf. 4(4), 2004, pp. 1-19.

[20] M. Shamsfard and A. Abdollahzadeh Barforoush, "Learning Ontologies from Natural Language Texts" International Journal of Human-Computer Studies archive Volume 60 Issue 1, January 2004 Article in a conference proceedings:

[21] L.F. Soualmia, C. Golbreich, and S.J. Darmoni, "Representing the MeSH in OWL: Towards a Semi-Automatic Migration" Conference: KR-MED 2004, First International Workshop on Formal Biomedical Knowledge Representation, Proceedings of the KR 2004 Workshop on Formal Biomedical Knowledge Representation, Whistler, BC, Canada, 1 June 2004, p. 9.

[22] A. Caruso, A. Folino, F. Parisi and R. Trunfio, "A statistical method for minimum corpus size determination" Proceedings of the 12es Journées internationales d'Analyse statistique des Données Textuelles (JADT 2014), pp. 135-146.

[23] D. Kless and S. Milton, "Towards Quality Measures for Evaluating thesauri" Metadata and semantic research. 4th international conference, MTSR 2010, Alcalá de Henares, Spain, October 20–22, 2010, pp. 312-319.

[24] E. Cardillo, A. Folino, R. Trunfio, and R. Guarasci, "Towards the reuse of standardized thesauri into ontologies", in Proceeding WOP'14 Proceedings of the 5th International Conference on Ontology and Semantic Web Patterns - Volume 1302, 2014, pp.26-37.

[25] F. Dell'Orletta, G. Venturi, A. Cimino and S. Montemagni, "T2K^2: a System for Automatically Extracting and Organizing Knowledge from Texts". In Proceedings of 9th Edition of International Conference on Language Resources and Evaluation (LREC 2014), 26-31 May, Reykjavik, Iceland, 2014.

[26] Informatics and Telematics Institute – National Council of Research, IIT – CNR, https://www.iit.cnr.it [accessed October 2018]

Extended Functionality of Mathematical Formulae Search Service

Alexander Gusenkov, Polina Gusenkova,
Yana Palacheva
IVMiIT, Kazan Federal University
Kazan, Russia
e-mails: alexandr.gusenkov@kpfu.ru
{polinagpa, palachevayana}@gmail.com

Olga Zhibrik
Gradient Technology Ltd
Kazan, Russia
e-mail: olgazhibrik@gmail.com

Abstract—**This paper focuses on the Mathematical Formulae Search Service of the Lobachevskii-DML (Digital Mathematical Library) project. The service is based on the original method of mathematical document markup that allows establishing relations among terms, variables, and formulae. This method was tested in two different search services with different preprocessing approaches. In Lobachevskii-DML, the instances of the mathematical entities are elicited as ontology concepts. The search service enables the user to seek formulae by textual definitions of their variables by generating ontology queries in SPARQL (SPARQL stands for SPARQL Protocol and RDF Query Language, RDF is the Resource Description Framework). The paper provides an overview of the search service and discusses the dynamic generation of the queries in response to new functionality features, including seeking formulae by more than one ontology concept.**

Keywords-semantic search; mathematical knowledge; ontology; formulae markup.

I. INTRODUCTION

The well-known phenomenon of the rapid increase in the amount of published information in many scientific fields has led to a growth of interest towards the subject of information structuring. The ongoing global digitalization of all the existing hard copy sources makes the research in this field even more important. Usually, scientific documents have a specific structure which is defined by the field. In case of mathematical documents, the text contains formulae, symbolic notations, and terms for the entities of the field. In terms of context, mathematical texts can be divided into theorems, axioms, proofs, mathematical definitions, etc. The most common digital representation of mathematical knowledge are papers written in LaTeX language.

Kazan Federal University is working on a project called Lobachevskii-DML, which can be considered a part of the World Digital Mathematical Library (WDML) project [1]-[3]. The WDML project is focused on digitalization and organization of the entire mathematical knowledge in an accessible and efficient way. Within the project, the information is represented through a system of mathematical objects stored in a specially organized repository. This paradigm has seen many implementations so far in the form of local and, in some way, limited DML projects all over the world, e.g., "All-Russian Mathematical Portal Math-Net.RU" [4], "Centre de diffusion de revues académiques mathématiques" [5], "Czech Digital Mathematics Library" [6].

Lobachevskii-DML is a digital mathematical library based on the mathematical knowledge management system OntoMath, which consists of ontologies, textual analytics tools, and applications for mathematical knowledge management [7]-[9]. The semantic search service is an important part of this project; it provides an interface to seek mathematical formulae containing variables that denote predetermined mathematical concepts.

This paper explains the fundamental principles of the markup method used for mathematical documents and the proposed formulae search algorithm [10]. The implementation of the search service based on this algorithm is also discussed, as well as the solution to an efficient formulae search by more than one ontology concept.

The rest of the paper is structured as follows. Section II covers the existing work and compares it with the proposed search method. Section III contains an overview of the Lobachevskii-DML project structure and some details on document processing and ontologies. Section IV outlines the core idea of an original Formula Markup Method. Section V provides details on the accuracy evaluation of the relations established during the document processing. Section VI includes the general description of the search service, as well as of the proposed new features. Section VII focuses on the solution to the implementation of the named features. The results of the search service modification are shown in Section VIII. Section IX covers current results and future possibilities.

II. STATE OF THE ART

Specialized search services that allow seeking information within specific collections of documents, such as scientific articles, is a fast-evolving research area. There are various systems that implement full-text search by keywords and narrow the search to scientific materials. Among these systems are well-known Google Scholar [11] and Microsoft Academic Search [12]. At the same time, a number of researches focus on implementations that allow making queries in LaTeX markup language: Springer LaTeXSearch [13], (uni)quation [14], EgoMath [15], MIaS [16], Wolfram Formula Search [17]. Some of the mentioned systems implement both approaches, for example, EgoMath allows to formulate search queries alternatively in LaTeX or natural language. However, such systems do not take into account the fact that new and specialized research areas do not often use well-established notations, and different scientific schools may use notations of their own. Lexical terminology is usually more consistent.

The novelty of our approach consists in the integration of the main functionalities of both full-text and formulae search by allowing the user to search for formulae using keywords in natural language. Instead of using mathematical expressions in a query, our approach allows using the textual names of variables that belong to the targeted formula. The search results in a formula and the text fragments which comprise variables and their textual definitions irrespective of their position in the text. Thereby, this approach integrates the functionalities of both full-text search and the search based on seeking a formula by its LaTeX fragments.

III. LOBACHEVSKII-DML

Lobachevskii-DML is built on the digital ecosystem OntoMath [18] which comprises ontologies, textual analytics tools, and applications for mathematical knowledge management. This system consists of the following components:

- Mocassin, an ontology of structural elements of mathematical scholarly papers;
- OntoMath^{PRO}, an ontology of mathematical knowledge concepts;
- Semantic publishing platform;
- Semantic formula search service;
- Recommender system.

The core component of the OntoMath ecosystem (see Figure 1) is its Semantic Publishing Platform. It takes a collection of mathematical articles in LaTeX as an input and builds their semantic representation, which includes metadata, the logical structure of documents, mathematical terminology and formulae.

Mocassin [19], an ontology of structural elements of mathematical papers, is used to identify specific segments, for example, a theorem, a proof, a formula (15 concepts in total). The ontology also defines relations between these segments.

The OntoMath^{PRO} [7][20] concepts are organized into two taxonomies: hierarchy of areas of mathematics, including its sub-fields; hierarchy of mathematical objects such as a set, function, integral, Fourier series, etc. This ontology defines the following relations: taxonomic relation, logical dependency, the associative relation between objects, belongingness of objects to fields of mathematics, the associative relation between problems and methods. The ontology concepts contain labels, definitions, links to external resources and relations to other concepts, as well as formulae and the relevant text fragments describing variables in these formulae. The terminological sources used during the development of the ontology are classical textbooks, online resources like Wikipedia and Cambridge Mathematical Thesaurus, scholarly papers, and personal experience of practicing mathematicians at Kazan Federal University.

Mocassin and OntoMath^{PRO} ontologies are parts of OntoMath ecosystem, however, SALT (Semantically Annotated LaTeX) [21] and AKT Portal (AKTive Portal created by the Advanced Knowledge Technologies research group) [22] are external ontologies.

To be included in Lobachevskii-DML, every article goes through several stages of processing. At the stage of structural markup, the document is annotated with generic structural elements such as titles, paragraphs, sentences, etc. Then, the formulae markup is performed, each expression is classified and some are linked to the text fragments which represent mathematical entities. The instances of the mathematical entities are elicited as the concepts of OntoMath^{PRO} ontology. The semantic search service uses the ontology concepts to provide means for seeking mathematical formulae that contain notations for these concepts.

The Semantic Formula Search is built using the Semantic Publishing Platform and implements an original formula markup method.

IV. FORMULA MARKUP METHOD

In mathematical texts, we identify the following three entities: *mathematical terms, symbolic notations for terms (variables)*, and *mathematical fragments (formulae)*. For a mathematical term, we use a Noun Phrase (NP) acting as an extended syntactic model.

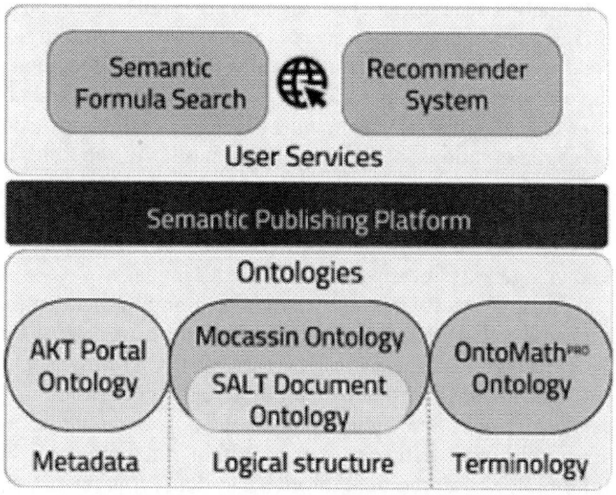

Figure 1. OntoMath ecosystem architecture

Relations among the mentioned entities are defined as follows. The first relation *terms - variables* is a textual definition of a symbolic notation through scientific terms within a certain context. The second relation *variables - formulae* indicates that a formula contains the symbolic notation. We assume that the appearance of the textual definition of a variable in the neighborhood of its symbolic representation points to a semantic relation between them. The idea of Maximum Permitted Distance (MPD) is used to determine this neighborhood. It is the distance in symbols to the left and to the right of the term which limits the area where a variable can be located. The context of the formula is formed by all the listed entities and relations between them.

The first implementation of the method was a search system for the Russian Wikipedia [23]. The system was based on full-text search within Wikipedia articles containing formulae. That implementation has demonstrated a working efficiency of the method. However, the full-text search focuses on the syntactic features of the searched terms instead of the semantic ones, which leads to a decrease in relevance in the case when the term is a part of some complex term. In order to solve this problem, the second implementation of the method uses preliminary semantic markup.

The formula markup method used in Lobachevskii-DML comprises two steps:

Step 1. Classification of Mathematical Expressions (ME). ME is considered as a *Math*-annotated text. ME consists of symbols for arithmetical and logical operators, variables, variables with index, keywords, and numbers. ME is classified as a *variable* in case it only consists of a variable or a variable with index. Otherwise, it is classified as a *formula*.

Step 2. Establishing relations between variables and formulae. For each *variable*, we search for its occurrences in every *formula* of the document:

Let $\{F\}$ be a set of formulae and $\{P\}$ be a set of variables.

$\forall$ p_i □ P, if p_i □ f_k □ F, the relation $<p_i,f_k>$ is established.

For each relation, the positions of the formula and variables in the text are stored as an attribute. This results in many-to-many relations between formulae and their variables (see Figure 2).

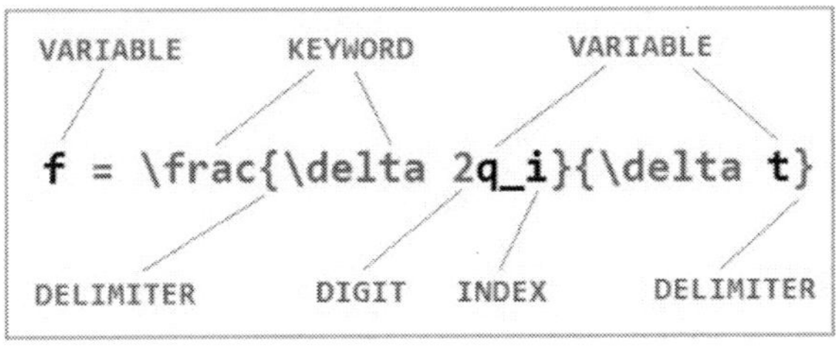

Figure 2. The structure of a mathematical formula.

In Step 1, the *Math*-annotated text is cleared from the service characters of the markup language and excessive space symbols. Next, the fragment is checked against a number of criteria (the length, the number of variables, the presence of relative operators and operations). If the fragment complies with the main criteria, it is considered a formula (a variable or any other type, for example, a table).

When constructing relations between formulae and variables, it is important to pay attention to unique variables in a formula which makes the formula analysis much easier (as opposed to full parsing). Regular expressions are used as a tool for the analysis. First, a formula is split into separate fragments. The delimiters are different types of braces, symbolic notations for arithmetical and logical operations, punctuation characters, spaces, etc. These fragments are then analyzed for belonging to a certain group - keywords (starting with “\”), lower indices (starting with “_”), numbers, etc. If the fragment is not classified at this stage, then it is very likely a single variable. The variables previously found in the text are compared to the variables found in formulae, and at Step 2, the relations of entries of the variables into formulae are established.

V. THE ACCURACY EVALUATION

To assess the accuracy of established relations among mathematical expressions and noun phrases, we used the set of articles from the magazine Izvestiya VUZ Matematika from years 1997-2009. All the articles in Lobachevskii-DML have resulted in 854284 RDF triplets; descriptions of 4190 theorems, 1015 definitions, etc. were included as well. The accuracy was manually evaluated by experts: the relations established with the proposed algorithm were compared to the expected results. The assessment was based on the assumption that the presence of incorrect relations causes irrelevant entries in search results. Besides, the relations that were expected but were never established would not be available for the search service.

Two collections of mathematical documents were processed to evaluate the following parameters:

- correctly related (CR) entities;
- correctly unrelated (CU) entities (which means that there is no NP definition within the context of ME);
- incorrectly related (IR) formulae and NPs (either the NP is semantically irrelevant or a relation was established within unfit context).

The results show that the percentage of correctly processed formulae (*CR+CU*) and the percentage of errors (*IR*) vary marginally in response to changing MPD (about 6% for MPD in a range from 15 to 40 symbols). At the same time, the evaluated parameters are changing non-linearly, which means that it is possible to find the most effective MPD for each set of documents. These experiments confirm the stability of the chosen algorithm. For the chosen document collection, the most effective MPD is 20 symbols; the percentage of correct relations is 67.84% (see Figure 3).

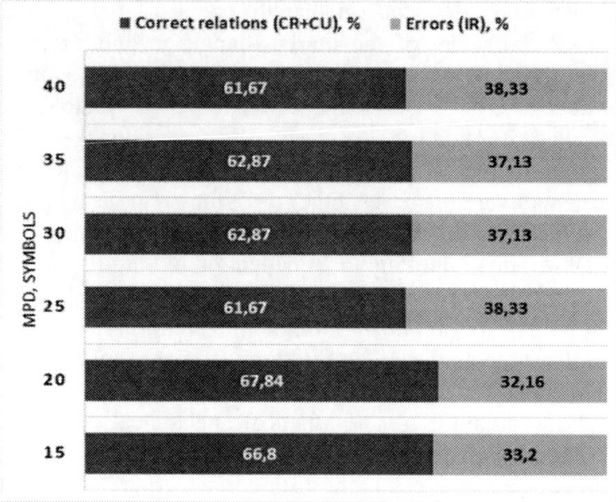

Figure 3. The accuracy of established relations

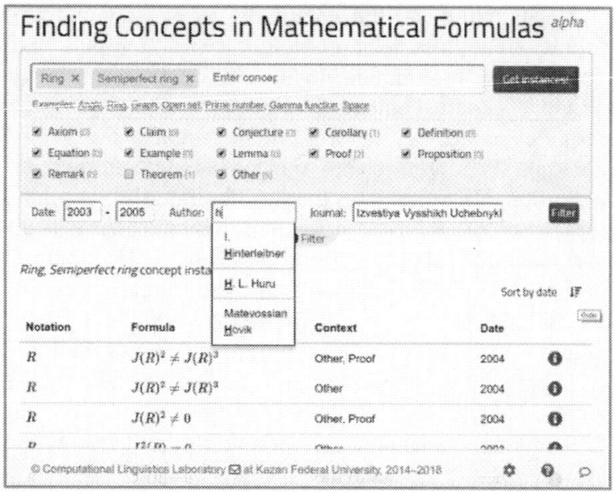

Figure 4. The modified interface of the search service.

VI. Semantic Search Service

After being automatically processed by the formula markup application, the documents become available to the semantic search service [10][24][25] of Lobachevskii-DML system. This implementation is similar to a search by keywords since it does not depend on symbolic notations for a mathematical concept. Keywords are resolved in terms of OntoMath^{PRO} ontology, and the relations of the ontology are used to create a search query. The user is able to limit the search context, for example, search only in definitions or in theorem statements.

The search service is a Web application implemented in JavaScript which uses the RDF query language SPARQL [26] to form a query. The result of the search is represented as a table of contextual data (see Figure 4) which contains a list of data including the symbolic notation of the chosen concept (variable), relevant formula and the context, i.e., the part of the document where the formula was found, as well as the article metadata and its text in PDF.

The alpha version of the search service was released and is now available for testing [27]. Preliminary testing was evaluated by the experienced mathematicians of Kazan Federal University. We have considered their comments and remarks in the modified version of the search service. In particular, the following modifications were suggested:

- search for formulae by more than one ontology concept, which requires dynamically generated queries with many parameters (this feature would allow seeking formulae containing several variables related to the targeted concepts);
- perform additional filtration of the results by metadata of the documents (presetting the range for publication date, the author, the publishers, etc.).

Specific problems and the results of the implementation of these features are explained in the next sections of this paper.

VII. Dynamic Generation of SPARQL Queries

The implementation of both search by several ontology concepts and the filtration of the results by metadata requires dynamic generation of search queries. A query must be generated in real time in response to user actions given the fact that these actions can be diverse. The SPARQL query language in itself does not support dynamic generation of queries, thus, additional tools are required.

Even though such extension libraries exist in many variations, in case of complex queries with many parameters aiming a specific ontology structure it may be difficult to choose a suitable general-purpose tool. Several approaches to query generation were considered, among which are string concatenation, patterns and macros, and query processors such as Apache Jena ARQ (Automated Request to Query) [28]. In an effort to minimize the cost of time and memory resources for query performance, as well as to easily integrate new features in the existing search service, the decision was made towards string concatenation. This resulted in a simple, yet effective query generation process.

Another important issue that arises when generating queries with many input parameters is query performance optimization. The specifics of the SPARQL language influence the possible approaches to the optimization problem. For example, the modifier DISTINCT is a costly operator, however, SPARQL language provides the modifier FILTER, which allows subqueries usage for filtering conditions and returns a set of unique results. Thus, the usage of the modifier FILTER positively influences the execution speed of a query [29].

The search query implemented in the original version of the search service aimed at one concept only. The query conditions listed all possible relations between a variable and a formula and used the modifier FILTER to select all the relations belonging to the targeted concept. This type of query required a considerable improvement to be able to perform a search by several concepts.

The search service uses endpoint provided by Virtuoso SPARQL Query Service [30]. Virtuoso SPARQL Query Editor [31] was used for query prototyping, testing and debugging.

Figure 5 displays the structure of a search query in SPARQL that determines the connections among concepts, variables, and formulae. The conditions describing relations among formulae and variables take precedence. Then, certain independent conditions are imposed on each variable notation connected to a certain ontology concept (belonging to a class). Then, filters are applied to the class of the variables in such a way so each of the targeted concepts is linked to one of the variables of the formula. This ensures that the keywords are processed as an AND combination. The query also handles some parts of metadata to extract the publication date. The results are grouped by formula.

The execution speed of such a query is decent: 0.8, 1.5 and 2 seconds for one, two and three concepts respectively. The query results are stored in a JavaScript data model that stores formula ID and the document source, its context, variables, LaTeX representation; it also allows querying the complete metadata of the source. Thus, a full-featured base structure was ensured to prepare the data to further processing and display.

Considering the specific nature of the search system, as well as the importance of maintaining the balance between functionality and performance, the search was limited to maximum three concepts per query. This is due to the fact that every targeted variable in the formula has to be linked to an ontology concept. It means that the text containing the targeted formula must include the definition of the variable, and this definition must be recognized during the markup stage, so the relation can be established. As the accuracy of the established relations is influenced by many factors (e.g., comprehensiveness of the ontology, accuracy of noun phrase extraction, the writing style), the increase in the number of the targeted concepts leads to the limited set of formulae that can be potentially found when searching by several concepts. The relation among three variable types is quite sufficient to define the targeted formula in the given collection of the mathematical documents.

```
PREFIX moc: <http://cll.niimm.ksu.ru/ontologies/mocassin#>
SELECT ?formula ?notation0 ?notation1 GROUP_CONCAT(?segment, " ") ...
WHERE  {
    ?formula a moc:Formula;
               moc:hasPart ?notation0, ?notation1; ...
    ?notation0 a ?class0; ...
    ?notation1 a ?class1; ...
    FILTER ( str (?class0) = '...' && str (?class1) = '...')
} GROUP BY ?formula ?notation0 ?notation1 ...
```

Figure 5. The general structure of a search query for two concepts.

VIII. MODIFIED SEARCH SERVICE

The result of this work is an extended version of the Lobachevskii-DML search service (Figure 4). It allows seeking formulae in collections of mathematical documents by one or more ontology concepts. The implementation is based on jQuery [32], a fast and versatile JavaScript library that focuses on the interaction between JavaScript and HTML.

The extended version contains new features such as multiple tag input, a drop-down list of possible inputs containing all the relevant ontology concepts, and a list of possible contexts (which is defined by the Mocassin ontology). An extra panel (hidden by default) contains additional filters: range for publication date, search by a specific author and the publisher.

The implementation of the tag input with drop-down list uses Flexdatalist [33], an autocomplete plugin with multiple input support, so there is no need to perform multiple queries because the data is loaded at the application startup through a single SPARQL query. If the list of the concepts searched has not been changed, the usage of the JavaScript library Knockout [34] allows to avoid performing a new query and hide some of the search results when the user applies the context filter, i.e., only the results found in definitions and proofs are shown.

A search query performed by the service results in a table of contextual data containing the following columns:

- the notation of the variable corresponding to the targeted concept in the particular formula;
- the formula that contains the variable;
- the context of the document in which the formula was found;
- the publication date.

Additionally, the user is able to sort the results by publication date. The search results are grouped by formulae to decrease the redundancy of results. Each result provides an access to further information about the found formula including a list of its linked variables and the metadata of the document containing the formula with a link to the text in PDF (Figure 6).

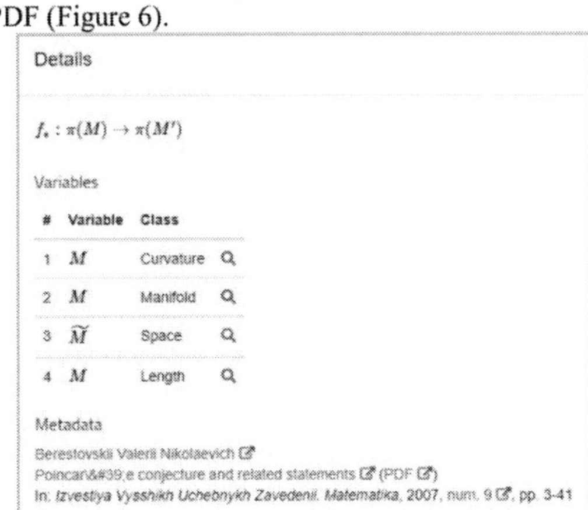

Figure 6. A window with detailed information for the formula.

Furthermore, some minor improvements of the interface were added: a back-to-top button, a search panel fixed to the top of the page that simplifies scrolling through the search results, and concept examples that perform an example search on click.

IX. Conclusions and Future Work

The semantic search service of the Lobachevskii-DML project combines both the convenience of a full-text search and the utility of formulae search. The terms of natural language query are translated into the variables checked for entry in the formulae. Based on the comments received during the preliminary user testing, several new features were implemented in order to make the interface more user-friendly. The challenges implied by the proposed features of the new functionality were solved successfully. As a result, there is an extended version of the Lobachevskii-DML semantic search service with considerable changes in the interface in the sense of both functionality and user experience.

The current version of the search service includes the following features:

- search by more than one concept (up to three), autocomplete for the input boxes, defining the context of the search (structural part of a document);
- access to full metadata on demand, filtration by metadata (date range, author, publisher), sorting by publication date;
- multi-language support (it is possible to search both in English and Russian).

Conducted tests of the extended search service showed stable results while retaining the previously achieved search relevance level (close to 68%). Search queries are generated and executed at a decent speed for the current data set. Preliminary user testing of the search results for one, two and three concepts allow us to conclude that the chosen approach was successful.

Future plans for development include further query generation and performance testing and optimization. It is worth considering the usage of text indexing for querying to make it more efficient. Additionally, the system is easily scalable with more features. More concepts can be available for searching, as the document collection is expanding. For further development, sorting search results by relevance may be considered.

The search service is currently in alpha-testing. The plans for improvement cover user interaction, as well as the algorithm of the system that defines the connections between formulae and ontology concepts and influences search relevance.

It should be noted that under this project we work on the recognition of mathematical documents in PDF which aids the development of the digital library. Handwritten text recognition is not the focus of our research; however, if some tools for digitizing such files and converting them into LaTeX format are available, it will be possible to include the resulting documents in the search service.

Acknowledgments

This work was funded by the subsidy allocated to Kazan Federal University for the state assignment in the sphere of scientific activities, grant agreement no. 1.2368.2018.

References

[1] Developing a 21st century global library for mathematics research, The National Academies Press, 2014.

[2] World Digital Mathematics Library (WDML), https://www.mathunion.org/ceic/library/ world-digital-mathematics-library-wdml, [retrieved: 2018.09.25].

[3] P. J. Olver, "The World Digital Mathematics Library: report of a panel discussion", Proceedings of the International Congress of Mathematicians, August 13–21, 2014, Seoul, Korea, vol. 1, pp. 773–785. Kyung Moon SA, 2014.

[4] All-Russian Mathematical Portal, http://www.mathnet.ru/, [retrieved: 2018.10.31].

[5] Center for diffusion of academic mathematical journals, http://www.cedram.org/, [retrieved: 2018.10.31].

[6] Czech Digital Mathematics Library, http://dml.cz/, [retrieved: 2018.10.31].

[7] O. Nevzorova, N. Zhiltsov, A. Kirillovich, and E. Lipachev, "OntoMath^PRO Ontology: A Linked Data Hub for Mathematics", Knowledge Engineering and the Semantic Web Communications in Computer and Information Science Volume 468, 2014, pp. 105-119, http://link.springer.com/chapter/10.1007/978-3-319-11716-4_9, arXiv:1407.4833, 2014.

[8] A. Elizarov et al., "Mathematical knowledge representation: semantic models and formalisms", Lobachevskii J. of Mathematics, 2014, 35, no 4, pp. 347–353.

[9] A. M. Elizarov, A. B. Zhizhchenko, N. G. Zhil'tsov, A. V. Kirillovich, and E. K. Lipachev, "Mathematical knowledge ontologies and recommender system for collections of documents in Physics and Mathematics", Computer Science, vol. 93, issue 2, pp. 231–233. Springer, Berlin, Heidelberg, 2016.

[10] E. Birialtsev, A. Gusenkov, O. Zhibrik, P. Gusenkova, and Y. Palacheva, "Search in Collections of Mathematical Articles", Á. Rocha, H. Adeli, L. P. Reis, and S. Costanzo (eds), Trends and Advances in Information Systems and Technologies. WorldCIST'18 2018. Advances in Intelligent Systems and Computing, vol. 745. Springer, Cham, 2018.

[11] Google Scholar, https://scholar.google.com, [retrieved: 2018.09.25].

[12] Microsoft Academic Search, http://academic.research.microsoft.com, [retrieved: 2018.09.25].

[13] The Springer LaTeX Search, http://latexsearch.com, [retrieved: 2018.09.25].

[14] (Uni)quation. Math expression search engine, http://uniquation.com, [retrieved: 2018.01.07].

[15] J. Misutka and L. Galambos, “Extending Full Text Search Engine for Mathematical Content”, Proceedings of DML, pp. 55–67, 2008.

[16] P. Sojka and M. Líška, “Indexing and Searching Mathematics in Digital Libraries”, J. H. Davenport, W. M. Farmer, J. Urban, and F. Rabe (eds), Intelligent Computer Mathematics. CICM 2011. Lecture Notes in Computer Science, vol 6824. Springer, Berlin, Heidelberg

[17] The Wolfram Functions Site, http://functions.wolfram.com, [retrieved: 2018. 09.25].

[18] A. Elizarov, A. Kirillovich, E. Lipachev, and O. Nevzorova, Digital Ecosystem OntoMath: Mathematical Knowledge Analytics and Management. In: L. Kalinichenko, S. Kuznetsov, and Y. Manolopoulos (eds) Data Analytics and Management in Data Intensive Domains. DAMDID/RCDL 2016. Communications in Computer and Information Science, vol 706. Springer, Cham

[19] V. Solovyev and N. Zhiltsov, “Logical structure analysis of scientic publications in mathematics”, Proceedings of the International Conference on Web Intelligence, Mining and Semantics (WIMS'11), 2011, pp. 21:1–21:9, ACM, 2011.

[20] E. V. Birialtsev et al., “Methods for Analyzing Semantic Data of Electronic Collections in Mathematics”, Automatic Documentation and Mathematical Linguistics, 2014, vol. 48, no. 2, pp. 81–85, 2014.

[21] T. Groza, S. Handschuh, K. Möller, and S. Decker, SALT - Semantically Annotated \LaTeX for Scientific Publications. In: Franconi E., Kifer M., May W. (eds) The Semantic Web: Research and Applications. ESWC 2007. Lecture Notes in Computer Science, vol. 4519. Springer, Berlin, Heidelberg

[22] The AKT Reference Ontology, http://projects.kmi.open.ac.uk/akt/ref-onto/, [retrieved: 2018.09.25]

[23] E. V. Birialtsev, A. M. Gusenkov, and O. N. Zhibrik, “Some approaches to markup of scientific texts containing mathematical expressions”, Uchenye Zapiski Kazanskogo Universiteta. Seriya Fiziko-Matematicheskie Nauki, 2014, vol. 156, no 4, pp. 133–148, 2014.

[24] A. Elizarov, A. Kirilovich, E. Lipachev, and O. Nevzorova, “Mathematical Knowledge Management: Ontological Models and Digital Technology”, CEUR Workshop Proceedings, 2016, vol. 1752, pp. 44-50, http://ceur-ws.org/Vol-1752/paper08.pdf, 2016.

[25] Finding Concepts in Mathematical Formulas alpha, http://lobachevskii-dml.ru:8890/mathsearch, [retrieved: 2018.09.25].

[26] SPARQL Query Language for RDF, v. 1.1, The W3C SPARQL Working Group, https://www.w3.org/TR/sparql11-overview/, [retrieved: 2018.09.25].

[27] Lobachevskii-DML search service, http://lobachevskii-dml.ru:8890/mathsearch, [retrieved: 2018.10.31].

[28] ARQ - A SPARQL Processor for Jena, https://jena.apache.org/documentation/query/, [retrieved: 2018.09.25].

[29] Bob DuCharme, “Learning SPARQL. Querying and Updating with SPARQL 1.1”, O'Reilly Media, 2013.

[30] Virtuoso SPARQL Query Service, http://vos.openlinksw.com/owiki/wiki/VOS/VOSSparqlProtocolVirtuoso, [retrieved: 2018.09.25].

[31] Virtuoso SPARQL Query Editor, http://lobachevskii-dml.ru:8890/sparql, [retrieved: 2018.09.25].

[32] jQuery, a JavaScript library, https://jquery.com/, [retrieved: 2018.10.31].

[33] Flexdatalist - jQuery autocomplete/datalist, http://projects.sergiodinislopes.pt/flexdatalist/, [retrieved: 2018.09.25].

[34] Knockout, http://knockoutjs.com/, [retrieved: 2018.09.25].

Tedi: a Platform for Ontologisation of Multilingual Terminologies for the Semantic Web

A Use Case from the Domain of Ancient Greek Cultural Heritage

Maria Papadopoulou[1,2], Christophe Roche[1,2]
1) Equipe Condillac « Terminology & Ontology » - Listic University Savoie Mont-Blanc, France
2) Knowledge Engineering & Terminology Research Centre University of Liaocheng, China
E-mail: firstname.lastname@univ-savoie.fr

Abstract- **The vision of the Semantic Web is machine understandability for all data currently stored in web-based resources. Terminological resources, which follow the ISO (International Organization for Standardization) standards on terminology in defining concepts as unique combinations of essential characteristics (ISO 1087-1), need to become computable and Semantic Web compliant. This paper, first, describes the theoretical approach and the tool-assisted method, which underlies the turning of these terminologies into Semantic web compliant ontologies. Next, this paper presents Tedi (ontoTerminology editor), the platform developed for building multilingual terminologies, which share the same formal domain ontology. Tedi allows to export these terminologies into OWL (Web Ontology Language), RDF (Resource Description Framework), JSON (JavaScript Object Notation), and in a number of other formats, including multilingual HTML (Hyper Text Markup Language) electronic dictionaries of terms. Tedi is based on a theory of concept dedicated to Terminology. Semantics is defined as the relation between terms (natural language units with meaning specialized to a domain of knowledge) and concepts (units of thought whose meaning is formally expressed as a set of essential characteristics), according to the discipline of Terminology. Tedi stores the linguistic and the conceptual dimensions in two related, yet distinct systems. This formal theory, which supplies the semantic onto-terminological layer needed for deeper data interpretability by machines, is less contrived and far more intuitive to use. It empowers domain experts to build their own semantic multilingual terminological dictionaries without having to be aware of logical formalisms like description logics. Semantic content management systems are direly needed in the domain of ancient cultural heritage. The remainder of the paper will illustrate this particular point with a use case from the domain of ancient Greek dress terminology presented from the point of view of the user (domain expert).**

Keywords- formal domain ontology; multilingual terminologies; ISO (and W3C (World Wide Web Consortium) standards; Tedi (ontoTerminology editor) software platform; ancient Greek cultural heritage.

I. INTRODUCTION

This paper proposes a tool-assisted method to design and create multilingual domain *ontoterminologies* (i.e., terminologies whose conceptual system is a formal domain ontology) relying on a definition of concept as a set of *essential characteristics*. An essential characteristic is such that, if removed from the object, the object is no more what it is, e.g., *mortal* for 'human being'). Such ontoterminologies are both ontologies that represent and model the concepts of a domain of specialized knowledge and terminologies that capture the verbal expression of this knowledge in different natural languages. The approach is based on the assumption that the same conceptualization of a specific domain can be shared across different linguistic communities, albeit expressed differently due to the difference in the linguistic medium. It follows that a formal domain ontoterminology can be built in order to capture a/ the conceptual layer of the domain of interest, and b/ the multilingual sets of terms denoting the concepts in the ontology. The concepts are defined in an artificial and formal language embedded in a user-friendly interface. The definitions of terms in natural language are built from the formal definitions of the concept each term denotes. This permits to guarantee some logical properties, such as coherence and completeness. What this achieves is a degree of standardization necessary for verbal communication among experts, inside and across communities of practice, based on a common understanding of their domain. This opens up new perspectives for the operationalization of terminologies for IT (Information Technology) applications. The approach is extremely useful for solving the problem of how to describe object-based knowledge of a part of the world in relation to the textual resources that refer to the same part, as is often the case in archaeology, classics, and cultural heritage studies.

The remainder of this paper is organized as follows: Section II describes the motivation that led to building the ontoterminology editor Tedi [1]. Section III presents related work and briefly explains why it is not sufficient. Section IV addresses the theoretical underpinnings of the ontoterminology approach. Section V describes the Tedi platform in terms of interfaces and details a use case from the domain of application. Our domain of choice was Greek dress, a domain which is deep-seated in modern perceptions of ancient Greek culture. The conclusions and future work section closes the article.

II. MOTIVATION

Ontologies and terminologies are at the core of the Semantic Web [2]. Ontologies, defined as "an explicit specification of a conceptualization" [3] mainly rely on description logics for their knowledge theory and on W3C interchange formats for their formal representation [4]. The dominant formalism for representing ontology has been the T-Box (assertions on concepts) and A-Box (assertions on individuals) in Description Logics (DL) (alias terminological logics [5]). "Concepts represent sets of individuals, roles represent binary relations between the individuals, and individual names represent single individuals in the domain. Readers familiar with first-order logic will recognize these as unary predicates, binary predicates and constants" [6]. Readers with no such background, however, will have difficulty grappling with the notion of DLs (Description Logics), better known for their decidability and the ability to infer additional knowledge, than for being intuitive [7]. The most popular free open-source editor for authoring ontologies based on these principles is Protégé [8] thanks to its powerful functionalities.

Not all terminologies rely on description logics for their conceptual system. Some terminologies follow the principles of the ISO standards for terminology work, which better match the way domain experts reason, because they are less contrived. There are numerous ISO standards for terminology work and no counterparts for dealing with ontology. The ISO 1087-1 and ISO 704, the standards on which all others should rely, were designed in times when the vision of the Semantic Web was not yet on the horizon (for a brief historical account see [9]). Their single goal was communication between humans, not IT applications [10], this is why they should be revised [11].

ISO 1087-1 [12] defines Terminology a/ as the "science studying the structure, formation, development, usage and management of terminologies in various subject fields", and b/ as the result of the application of this science to a dedicated specialized domain, i.e., a "set of designations belonging to one special language". ISO 1087-1 defines concept as a "unit of knowledge created by a unique combination of characteristics" and term as a "verbal designation of a general concept in a specific subject field". Representing concepts as sets of essential characteristics, not as sets of individuals (which is what Protégé does) allows to focus more on the *nature* of objects than on defining their properties solely as binary relations that link them together ("roles" in DLs, "slots" in Protégé). Based on Aristotelian definitions by *genus* and *differentia*, concepts can be verbalized in a more human readable form than restrictions on roles. This type of definition is particularly useful for ontology extraction [13]. What is more, a terminological system, which is also an ontology authoring tool with logic-based formalisms and adheres to W3C standards, is extremely useful to domain experts and terminologists who do not have background in logic, but need to build their own machine-actionable and understandable domain terminologies. Tedi, a new ontology editing platform for terminologies of a given domain, was born out of the drive to respond to these needs. Formalized terminologies are essential for language processing tasks, for reasoning upon the data, for the creation of fully computable multilingual dictionaries, and for connecting object-based with text-based resources.

III. Related Work

Relevant research on the state-of-the art on representing the semantics of our data for the Semantic web points towards the following directions:

A. Ontologisation of non-ontological resources

A conceptual model of a domain is at the core of most knowledge based systems and language processing systems. The specific contribution of formal ontologies is the detailed, logical definition of the concepts and of the possible semantic relations between entities. Today one of the most prominent application of ontologies is the semantic indexing of content for resource discovery. This requires that the underlying data has rich and unambiguous semantics. The need for structuring the categories of the domain in a way that can be communicated without the risks of natural language ambiguity and polysemy has given rise to numerous efforts to use controlled languages and vocabularies. For a relatively recent state-of-the-art see [14]-[15].

This approach is similar to that of wielding the power of thesauri as a less powerful and less granular way to structure into a hierarchy the terms of a domain. Thesauri structure concepts into monohierarchic trees or polyhierarchic lattices, ontologies structure them into semantically-rich directed graphs. The example of the ontologization of AGROVOC Thesaurus is a clear manifestation of the advantage of terminologically rich domain ontologies over other types of Knowledge Organization Systems (KOS) [16]. The current need to reengineer cultural heritage thesauri into ontologies is exemplified by Getty Vocabularies [17]-[18].

B. Building natural language interfaces for representing knowledge on the Semantic Web

Semantic Content Authoring and Linked Data authoring for user-friendly creation of content (manual or semi-automatic) on the web of data are rapidly emerging. Natural language interfaces support end users who are not computer experts. A range of capabilities such as the authoring of knowledge content, the retrieval of information from semantic repositories, and the generation of pattern for definitions in natural language make content management more intelligent through the injection of descriptive semantics in the process of content creation [19].

C. Building lexical models for the representation of lexical data on the Semantic Web

The primary mechanisms for the representation of lexical data on the Semantic Web has been the Lemon core model [20] (with extra modules for Syntax and Semantics, Decomposition, Variation and Translation, and Metadata [21]), further developed in the context of the W3C OntoLex community group into the new OntoLex-Lemon model [22].

D. Using existing ontology authoring environments

Before setting off, we considered using existing ontology editors. There exist different ontology editing tools, which support the creation and population of ontologies for the semantic web, but, to our knowledge, none which allows to directly take into account the notion of 'essential characteristic' for defining domain concepts. In order to build our domain ontology, we used Tedi, a software which empowers domain experts to do their own ontological modelling. We decided against building our ontology directly in Protégé, even though Protégé is a feature-rich open-source platform for the construction of ontologies for the semantic web and is supported by a big user community. Protégé users have to familiarize themselves with defining classes (concepts) in terms of roles and role restrictions, which is hardly intuitive for those with no background in Logic. Granted, modelling in Protégé is a steep learning curve for non-computer scientists [23]. In contrast, Tedi supports the definition of formal ontologies by means of *essential* and *descriptive characteristics*, which are more intuitive to domain experts. For example, *sewn* is an essential characteristic of the garment exomis, whereas *color* is a descriptive one. Unlike descriptive characteristic, essential characteristic cannot be assigned a value. Its formalization requires a higher logic. Furthermore, the notion of 'essential characteristic' is a cornerstone for Conceptual Terminology in Specialized Languages. Conceptual Terminology distinguishes the *definition* of concepts (set of essential characteristics) from the *description* of objects (set of descriptive characteristics).

E. Ontologising cultural heritage

Last, in order to ontologise our terminology from the cultural heritage of ancient Greece we considered using relevant ISO standards, especially the ISO 1087-1 standard on vocabulary, theory and application of terminology, and the ISO 704 on principles and methods of terminology work. As already discussed these ISO standards are not operationalisable [11]. There is one ISO standard for the cultural heritage sector, which as will be shown below, our approach aims to extend. The vocabulary for the description of cultural objects was accepted as international standard ISO 21127 and is also known as CIDOC-CRM (Conseil International des Musées-Conceptual Reference Model) [24]-[25]. CIDOC-CRM does not specifically address the terminologies of the cultural heritage domain [26]. The same holds for other data models used in the cultural heritage and museum community, e.g., LIDO (Lightweight Information Describing Objects) [27] and EDM (Europeana Data Model) [28].

Due to the semantic richness and heterogeneity of cultural content and the distributed ways in which this content is created by domain experts, cultural heritage is a field where semantic technologies should become the standard technology to use. While archaeology and classical studies have spearheaded the use of digital tools, they have been quite slow in adopting W3C standards, mainly due to the belief that the type of humanistic inquiry pursued in these fields cannot or should not be standardized [29]. The theory and practice of ontological representation and modelling of archaeological, and more broadly, cultural heritage material, needs to be informed by the epistemic traditions of the disciplines involved [30]. Models that capture information independently of linguistic and cultural variation can standardize this diversity by adding a formal layer to the data. Knowledge, even tacit knowledge, needs to be expressed in a language, either natural or artificial. Models to cover both the conceptual and the terminological aspects of this knowledge are definitely going to multiply in the near future [31] – [33].

In the domain of ancient Greek cultural heritage, efforts are made to produce new domain-specific standards, such as the standard for digital editions of texts inscribed on a range of materials, including stone and papyrus (EpiDoc, Epigraphic Documents in TEI-XML, Text Encoding Initiative - eXtensible Markup Language) [34], and the Standards of Networking Ancient Prosopographies (SNAP) [35]. Moreover, geo-ontologies, such as Pelagios [36] and Google Ancient Places [37] link space as place to ancient time, while datasets of ancient artefacts, such as coins [38] and pottery [39], can now be published as LOD (Linked Open Data). The formalization of terminological systems in the domain, however, remains at a nascent stage.

IV. The Ontoterminology Approach

The need to make terminologies that are meant for human communication machine-processible according to international de facto and de jure standards motivated the first machine-readable trilingual terminology of ancient Greek dress (in English, French, and Greek) [40]. Our approach set out to build a formal domain ontology and make the resulting structured data shareable on the web of data. To achieve this means dealing with the ambiguity of natural language in defining the concepts of the domain. A degree of formalization/standardization was achieved, first, by clearly distinguishing between the concept level (i.e., the stable domain knowledge) and the term level (i.e., the natural language that is used to name the domain concepts); second, by putting them into relation (i.e., linking the terms in different languages to their denoted concepts). This leads to combining ontology and terminology into the new paradigm of ontoterminology [41]. An additional objective was to create a tool that lowers the barrier for users not familiar with knowledge engineering, both at the technical level and at the level of the logical theory adopted. When exporting in OWL essential characteristics are translated into classes; essential characteristics belonging to the same axis of analysis, therefore mutually exclusive, are translated into disjoint classes. There are different ways of translating essential characteristics into OWL. The use of classes is one of them. It is also possible to simulate a second order logic in considering essential characteristics as individuals [42].

V. Tedi Software Platform

The Tedi software platform was developed in VisualWorks at the University Savoie Mont-Blanc [1]. It supports both term standardization and customization. Standardization of terminologies relies upon expert agreement on domain knowledge, which is necessary for collaboration and rapid sharing of information.

Tedi relies on a theory of concept inspired by the ISO standards on terminology. It is based on the notion of *essential characteristic*. The essential characteristics are grouped into *axes of analysis* (sets of exclusive essential characteristics, e.g., a garment can be either wrapped or attached; either worn directly on the skin or as an overgarment; etc.). The set of axes of analysis constitutes an 'orthogonal base' for the meaning of the concepts. The logical properties of the system are verified at every step of ontology building.

Such modelling of domain knowledge can be very finely structured knowledge in order to eventually support two types of queries: by means of words, and by means of concepts. In order to clearly distinguish between the different types of knowledge on which Tedi relies, we use the following conventions: concepts are written between angle brackets "< >", whereas essential characteristics (also called "differences" in Tedi) are written between slashes "/.../", and terms written between quotes "...". For example, the term "exomis" denotes a type of objects associated to the following set of characteristics: /for man/, /around body/, /more than one part/, /with sewing/, /without sleeves/, /attached/, /one attachment/, /knee-length/, /unpleated/, /under/.

A. Tedi Editors

Tedi's rich architecture deploys two interconnected systems for the conceptual and linguistic dimensions. The *concept editor* allows to define essential characteristics, axes of analysis, attributes (descriptive characteristics), relations, and concepts. It also allows to update the ontology by inserting new concepts into the hierarchy. In order to help structure the system, Tedi automatically infers the possible generic concepts as well as the possible essential characteristics. The system's in-built reasoner checks the compatibility of the essential characteristics in order to propose only those that are possible at a given moment. It also infers those that can be logically inferred and generates the formal definition of the concept, helping the expert to manage the combinatorial explosion (n axes of analysis made up of two exclusive essential characteristics potentially define 2^n concepts). If there is no concept corresponding to the set of essential characteristics denoted by a term, Tedi proposes to create a new concept and a new concept name based on the selected essential characteristics.

In the *term editor*, the user can: enter the terms in as many languages as needed, declare the status for each term (term status can be parameterized) and the part-of-speech for each term (choosing from: noun, verb, adjective, none), add contexts and notes. Tedi generates a pattern of definition for each term on the basis of the formal definition of the denoted concept. The system also calculates automatically the *terminological equivalents* across different languages, but also in a given language and for a given term the *terminological synonyms*, *terminological hypernyms* and *hyponyms* (two terms are *terminological synonyms* if and only if they denote the same concept).

B. Export Formats

Tedi enables domain experts to capture domain knowledge, to express it formally regardless of their background in formal languages, and to export it into different formats, which, of course, are not equivalent. At its present version (version 1.1) Tedi exports in CSV (Comma Separated Values), HTML (both static and dynamic), JSON, and RDF / OWL.

C. Use case: Conceptualizing Ancient Greek Garments

In the use case we present here the user needs to define the Greek dress multilingual ontoterminology. Figure 1 shows a screenshot of the modelling of the garment termed "ἐξωμίς" in ancient Greek, "exomis" in English and "exomide" in French. Textual and iconographic evidence has shown that the "exomis" is a male unpleated and sleeveless garment that covers the body down to the knees and is attached at one point of attachment.

The ontoterminology building process, centered on essential characteristics, consists in five interrelated non-linear iterative tasks that the expert should take for every concept defined in the system.

Task 1: Go to Tedi Term editor: enter the terms to be defined in the language(s) we need. These terms can be given directly by the experts or from NLP tools for candidate term extraction. Define their Status (choosing from the following drop-down list: preferred, alternative, tolerated, not recommended, obsolete), and their PoS (Part-of-Speech) (choosing from: noun, verb, adjective, none).

Task 2: In Tedi Concept editor: define the essential characteristics and the axes of analysis. These essential characteristics are found out by identifying differences between objects.

Task 3: In Tedi Term editor: link the term to the concept. Select all the essential characteristics that you want associated with the term. If there is no corresponding concept, Tedi proposes to create a new one, whose name is constructed from the chosen essential characteristics. The set of characteristics that have been selected is its formal definition, i.e., its definition in a formal language imbedded in Tedi. The axes of analysis, their dependencies and the compatibility of the essential characteristics are managed by Tedi. The system automatically checks the compatibility of the defined essential characteristics thus guiding the expert by proposing only those that are possible at a given moment.

Task 4: In Tedi Concept editor: update the ontology by inserting the newly created concept into the conceptual system, i.e., by linking it hierarchically (or associatively) with other concepts, supplementing its description by the addition of descriptive characteristics, if necessary. Where appropriate, new concepts can be introduced for the purposes of organizing the conceptual system without there being any terms that designate them in the given linguistic system. In order to help structure the system, Tedi automatically infers the possible generic concepts for a given concept, i.e., their intensional definitions, consisting in all their essential characteristics, are included in the intensional definition of the concept.

Task 5: In Tedi Term editor: complete the definition of terms in different languages. To this end, Tedi proposes 'patterned' definitions in natural language on the basis of the formal definition of the concept denoted by the term and its terminological hypernym. It remains for the expert to reformulate them syntactically and put them in their final form.

D. Validation

Going back to the example, the concept denoted by the term "exomis" is defined by the characteristics: /for man/, /around body/, /more than one part/, /with sewing/, /without sleeves/, /attached/, /one attachment/, /knee-length/, /unpleated/, /under/. This set of features constitutes the formal definition of the concept. Tedi automatically infers that this concept counts <Garment around body> and <Garment for man> among its possible generic concepts. The concept name proposed by Tedi is a concatenation of these characteristics: < Garment for man around body more than one part with sewing without sleeves attached one attachment knee-length unpleated under >. The definition for the term 'exomis' in English is: "Short and non-pleated garment for man, usually worn around the body directly on the skin, this sleeveless garment consists of two sewn pieces of cloth, attached on the left shoulder leaving naked the right shoulder and part of the chest". The Greek-English Lexicon, also known as LSJ (Liddell Scott Jones), which is the standard dictionary for scholarly use defines exomis as "tunic with one sleeve". A mere comparison of the two definitions illustrates the usefulness of the essential characteristics approach.

VI. CONCLUSION & FUTURE WORK

To sum up, this paper presented a tool-assisted method for the ontologization of terminologies meant for human communication, so that they become interpretable also by machines. The approach and software presented here reflect the need for deeper semantics in the ontological part of a representation of reality, so that the represented part and the specialized language for human use can be more fully interpreted by machines. Tedi can be used to create multilingual terminological dictionaries of a domain containing definitions for terms in natural language, their canonical and inflected forms, and a wealth of related unstructured data in the form of notes, contexts of use, images, and videos. By combining ontology, terminology, and user-friendliness, Tedi software offers the possibility to enrich text-based data through semantic annotations. Ontoterminologies can be exported into different interchange formats including JSON and OWL. An ontoterminology mashup and server is currently under way.

ACKNOWLEDGMENT

We gratefully acknowledge the generous funding of the European Commission Marie Skłodowska-Curie (grant agreement no. 657898).

REFERENCES

[1] http://ontoterminology.com/tedi [retrieved: 09/2018]

[2] https://www.w3.org/standards/semanticweb/ [retrieved: 09/2018]

[3] T. Gruber, "A Translation Approach to Portable Ontology Specifications". Knowledge Acquisition, vol. 5, no. 2, pp. 199-220, 1993.

[4] F. Baader, D. Calvanese, D. McGuinness, D. Nardi, P. Patel-Schneider, The Description Logic Handbook. Cambridge: Cambridge University Press, 2003.

[5] B. Nebel, "Frame-based systems," in The MIT Encyclopedia of the Cognitive Sciences, R. A. Wilson and F. C. Keil, Eds. Cambridge, MA: MIT Press, pp. 324-325, 1991.

[6] J. Quantz and M. Ryan, Preferential Default Description Logics. KIT report 110, Berlin, 1993.

[7] M. Dzbor and E. Motta, "Engineering and Customizing Ontologies. Ontology Management". Semantic Web, Semantic Web Services, and Business Applications, Semantic Web and Beyond. Computing for Human Experience, vol. 7, Berlin, Springer, pp. 25-57, 2008.

[8] https://protege.stanford.edu/ [retrieved: 09/2018]

[9] http://www.infoterm.info/standardization/history_standardization_terminological_principles_and_methods.php [retrieved: 09/2018]

[10] ISO 704:2009 Terminology work – Principles and methods.

[11] C. Roche, "Should Terminology Principles be re-examined?", 10th Terminology and Knowledge Engineering Conference, Madrid, Spain, 19-22 June 2012, pp. 17-32, 2012.

[12] ISO 1087-1:2000 Terminology work – Vocabulary – Part 1.

[13] D. Poole and A. Mackworth. Artificial Intelligence. Foundations of Computational Agents, Cambridge: Cambridge University Press, 2010.

[14] H. Safwat and B. Davis, "CNLs for the semantic web: a state of the art," Lang. Resour. Eval., vol. 51, no. 1, March 2017, pp. 191-220, 2017.

[15] T. Kuhn, "A survey and classification of controlled natural languages". Computational Linguistics 40, 1, March 2014, pp. 121-170, 2014.

[16] D. Soergel, B. Lauser, A. Liang, F. Fisseha, J. Keiser, S. Katz, "Reengineering Thesauri for New Applications: the AGROVOC Example," Journal of Digital Information, vol. 4, no. 4: New Applications of KOS, 2004.

[17] D. Soergel, "The Art and Architecture Thesaurus (AAT): A critical appraisal," Visual Resources, X, pp. 369-400, 1995.

[18] J. Cobb, "The Journey to Linked Open Data: The Getty Vocabularies", Journal of Library Metadata vol., 15, no. 3-4, pp. 142-156, 2015.

[19] A. Crapo and A. Moitra, "Towards a unified English-like representation of semantic models, data, and graph patterns for subject matter experts" International Journal of Semantic Computing, vol. 7, no. 3, pp. 215-236, 2013.

[20] https://lemon-model.net/ [retrieved: 09/2018]

[21] M. Fiorelli, A. Stellato, J. P McCrae, P. Cimiano, M. T. Pazienza, "LIME. The Metadata Module for ONTOLEX", in Proceedings of 12th Extended Semantic Web Conference. Springer International Publishing, H. Sack Ed., pp. 321-336, 2015.

[22] J. P. McCrae, J. Bosque-Gil, J. Gracia, P. Buitelaar, P. Cimiano, "The OntoLex-Lemon Model: development and applications," pp. 587-597, 2017.

[23] M. Horridge et al., "Simplified OWL ontology editing for the web: is WebProtégé enough?" The Semantic Web - ISWC 2013, Proceedings part I - 12th International Semantic Web Conference, Sydney, Australia, pp. 200-215, 2013.

[24] http://www.cidoc-crm.org/ [retrieved: 09/2018]

[25] http://erlangen-crm.org/ [retrieved: 09/2018]

[26] M. Doerr, "The CIDOC conceptual reference module: an ontological approach to semantic interoperability of metadata," AI Mag. 24, 3, September 2003, pp. 75-92, 2003.

[27] http://network.icom.museum/cidoc/working-groups/lido/lido-technical/specification/Europeana Data Model version 5.2.7-25/04/2016 [retrieved: 09/2018]

[28] https://pro.europeana.eu/resources/standardization-tools/edm-documentation [retrieved: 09/2018]

[29] M. Doerr, Ontologies for Cultural Heritage. Handbook on Ontologies, second edition. In S. Staab and R. Studer, Eds., Springer: Cham, Switzerland, pp. 463-480, 2009.

[30] C. Dallas, "Archaeological knowledge, virtual exhibitions and the social construction of meaning." Archeologia e Calcolatori, vol. 18, pp. 31-64, 2007.

[31] O. Signore, "The Semantic Web and Cultural Heritage: Ontologies and technologies help in accessing museum information," in Information Technology for the Virtual Museum, Sønderborg, Denmark, 2006.

[32] S. Hai-Jew, Semantic Web for Cultural Heritage Valorisation in Data Analytics in Digital Humanities, Springer: Cham, Switzerland, 2017.

[33] K. N. Vavliakis, G. Th. Karagiannis, P. A. Mitkas, "Semantic Web in Cultural Heritage After 2020," in Proceedings of What will the Semantic Web look like 10 years from now? Workshop held in conjunction with the 11th International Semantic Web Conference 2012 (ISWC 2012), Nov. 7-11, Boston, MA, 2012. http://issel.ee.auth.gr/wp-content/uploads/2016/02/Semantic-Web-in-Cultural-Heritage-After-2020.pdf [retrieved: 09/2018]

[34] http://epidoc.sf.net [retrieved: 09/2018]

[35] http://snapdrgn.net [retrieved: 09/2018]

[36] http://commons.pelagios.org/ [retrieved: 09/2018]

[37] https://googleancientplaces.wordpress.com/ [retrieved: 09/2018]

[38] http://nomisma.org/ontology [retrieved: 09/2018]

[39] http://kerameikos.org/ontology [retrieved: 09/2018]

[40] M. Papadopoulou and C. Roche, "Ontoterminology of ancient Greek garments", Toth 2017, Terminology & Ontology: Theories and applications, Chambéry, France, 8-9 June 2017. pp. 73-92, 2018.

[41] C. Roche, "Ontoterminology: How to unify terminology and ontology into a single paradigm," LREC 2012, 8th international conference on Language Resources and Evaluation, Istanbul, Turkey, 21-27 May 2012, pp. 2626-2630, 2012.

[42] M. Spies and C. Roche, "Aristotelian Ontologies and OWL Modeling," Handbook of Ontologies for Business Interaction. Information Science Reference, Hershey: New York, pp. 21-33, 2008.

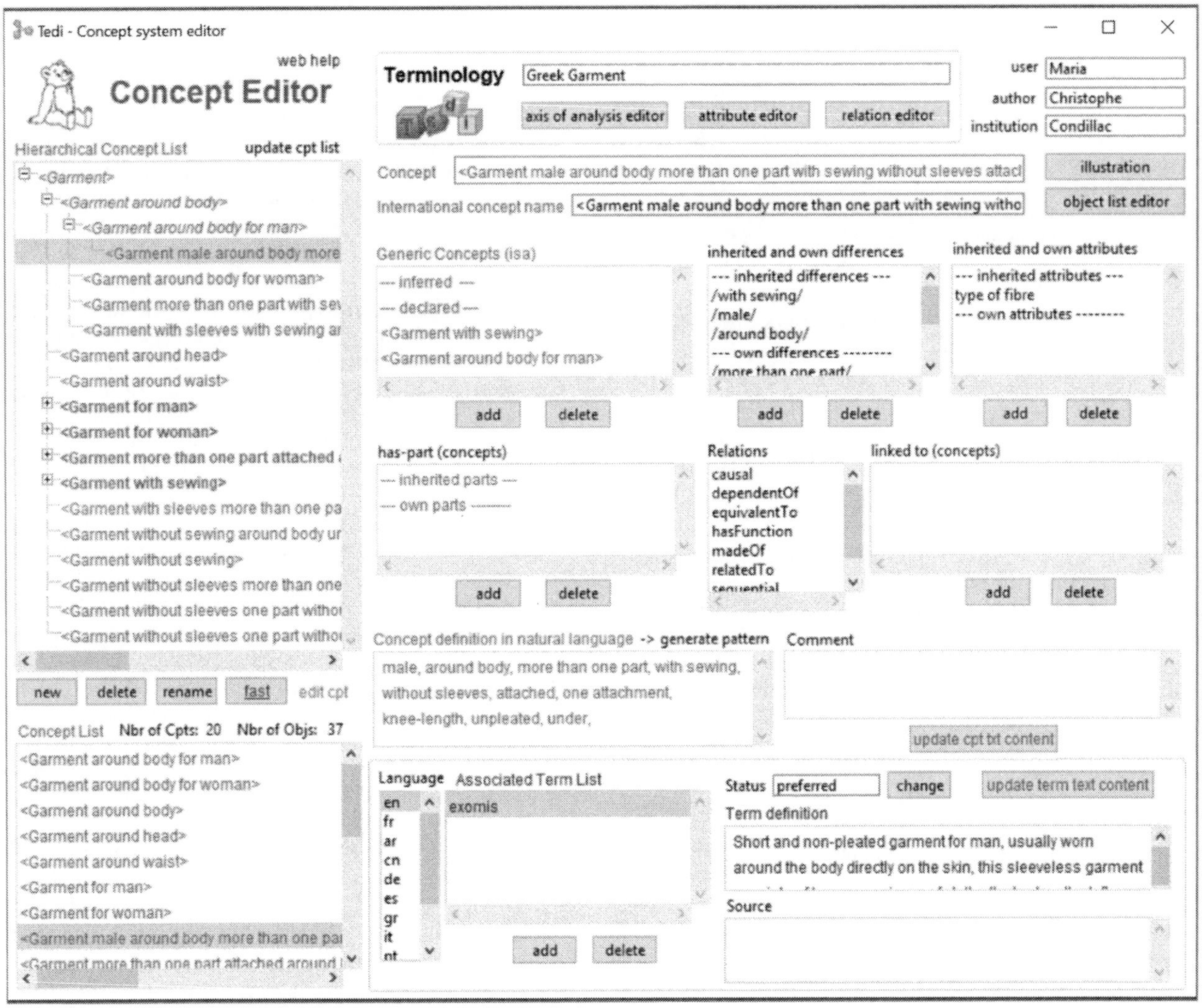

Figure 1. Modelling the conceptual dimension for example domain concept denoted by term "exomis" in Tedi Concept Editor.

Estimating Semantic Similarity for Targeted Marketing based on Fuzzy Sets and the Odenet Ontology

Tim vor der Brück

School of Information Technology
Lucerne University of Applied Sciences and Arts
Rotkreuz, Switzerland
e-mail: tim.vorderbrueck@hslu.ch

***Abstract*—Estimating the semantic similarity between texts is of vital importance for a wide range of application scenarios in natural language processing. With the increasing availability of large text corpora, data-driven approaches like Word2Vec became quite successful. In contrast, semantic methods, which employ manually designed knowledge bases like ontologies lost some of their former popularity. However, manually designed knowledge can still be a valuable resource, since it can be leveraged to boost the performance of data-driven approaches. We introduce in this paper a novel hybrid similarity estimate based on fuzzy sets that exploits both word embeddings and a lexical ontology. As ontology we use Odenet, a freely available resource recently developed by the Darmstadt University of Applied Sciences. Our application scenario is targeted marketing, in which we aim to match people to the best fitting marketing target group based on short German text snippets. The evaluation showed that the use of an ontology did indeed improve the overall result in comparison with a baseline data-driven estimate.**

Keywords–Odenet; Fuzzy sets; Targeted marketing; Histogram equalization.

I. INTRODUCTION

Market segmentation is one of the key tasks of a marketer. Usually, it is accomplished by clustering over demographic variables, geographic variables, psychographic variables and behaviors [1]. In this paper, we will describe an alternative approach based on unsupervised natural language processing. In particular, our business partner operates a commercial youth platform for the Swiss market, where registered members get access to third-party offers such as discounts and special events like concerts or castings. Actually, several hundred online contests per year are launched over this platform sponsored by other firms, an increasing number of them require the members to write short free-text snippets, e.g., to elaborate on a perfect holiday at a destination of their choice in case of a contest sponsored by a travel agency. Based on the results of a broad survey, the platform provider's marketers assume six different target groups (called *milieus*) being present among the platform members. For each milieu (with the exception of the default milieu *special groups*) a keyword list was manually created to describe its main characteristics. For triggering marketing campaigns, an algorithm has been developed that automatically assigns each contest answer to the most likely target group: we propose the youth milieu as best match for a contest answer, for which the estimated semantic similarity between the associated keyword list and user answer is maximal. For the estimation of text relatedness, we devised a novel semantic similarity estimate based on a combination of word embeddings and Odenet, where the latter is a freely available lexical ontology recently developed by the Darmstadt University of Applied Sciences.

There is a multitude of existing approaches to estimate text similarity by means of ontologies. Liu and Wang [2] match each word of a text to a concept in an ontology and derive a vector representation for it consisting of its weighted one hot-encoded hypernyms, hyponyms and the matched concept itself, where the weights are specified beforehand and assume the maximum value of 1 for the latter. An entire document can then be represented by the centroid vector of all words in the documents. As usual, the comparison with other documents can be accomplished by applying the cosine measure on the centroids. In contrast to Liu and Wang, Mabotuwana et al. [3] disregard the hyponyms for constructing the word vectors and set the weight of a hypernym to the inverse of the number of nodes on the shortest path in the ontology from the matched concept to this hypernym. A downside of this method is that simple path length count is quite unreliable in capturing semantic similarity, which is a finding of Resnik [4]. Therefore, he introduced the so-called information content (IC), which is the negative logarithm of the occurrence probability of a word and aims to compensate for differences of semantic similarities between nodes of taxonomy edges. The IC constitutes also the basis for several novel semantic similarity measures introduced by Lastra Díaz et al. [5], [6]. Mingxuan Liu and Xinghua Fan [7] propose to enrich texts with semantically related words (hypernyms) to improve the categorization of short Chinese texts, which is the approach, we want to follow here. But, in contrast to Mingxuan Liu and Xinghua Fan, we will not represent the words occurring in the texts by ordinary sets but instead by fuzzy sets, which allows us to incorporate word vectors in our similarity score. All the methods described so far return a single scalar value as similarity estimator. The approach of Oleshshuk and Pedersen however, derives a similarity vector, which represents the semantic similarities on different abstraction levels of the ontology as estimated by the Jaccard index [8].

An alternative method to estimate semantic similarity is the use of word embeddings. These embeddings are determined beforehand on a very large corpus typically using either the skip gram or the continuous bag of words variant of the Word2Vec model [9]. The skip gram method aims to predict the textual surroundings of a given word by means of an artificial neural network. The influential weights of the one-hot-encoded input word to the nodes of the hidden layer constitute the embedding vector. For the so-called *continuous bag of words* method, it is just the opposite, i.e., the center word is predicted by the words in its surrounding. Alternatives to Word2Vec are GloVe [10], which is based on aggregated global word co-occurrence statistics and the Explicit Semantic Analysis (ESA) [11], in which each word is represented by the column vector in the tf-idf matrix over Wikipedia. The idea of Word2Vec can be transferred to the level of sentences as well. In particular, the so-called Skip-Thought Vector model [12] derives a vector representation of the current sentence by predicting the surrounding sentences. Again, a similarity estimate can be obtained by applying the cosine measure on the embeddings centroids of the two documents to compare. There is some former work to devise similarity estimates combining ontologies and word embeddings. The approach of Faruqui et al. [13] aims to retrofit the embedding vectors in such a way that related words with respect to the employed ontology have preferably similar vector representations. Goikoetxea et al. [14] generate random walks on WordNet to extract sequences of concepts. These sequences are then fed into the ordinary Word2Vec to create (ontology) embeddings vectors. They evaluated several possibilities to combine such vectors with word embeddings like averaging or concatenating them. A downside of this approach in comparison with our proposed estimate is that at least one million of such random walks must be generated to obtain sufficiently reliable results. So, the required format conversion, which needs to be repeated for every change in the ontology, is quite time-consuming.

The remainder of this paper is organized as follows: Our proposed methodology is described in Section II. Section III introduces the Odenet ontology and compares it with GermaNet. In Section IV we investigate, how similarity estimates can be combined that exhibit very different probability distributions. The evaluation is contained in Section V. Finally, we conclude the paper in Section VI with an overview of the accomplished results and possible future work.

II. Proposed Methodology

A straight-forward and simple method to estimate the similarity between two texts is applying the Jaccard index on their bag of words representations [15]. This coefficient is given as:

$$jacc(A,B) = \frac{|A \cap B|}{|A \cup B|} \qquad (1)$$

where A (B) is the set of words of the first (second) text. While this approach works reasonably well for long texts, it usually fails for short text snippets since in this case it is very likely that all overlaps are caused by very common words (typical stop words), which are actually irrelevant for estimating text similarity. One possibility to increase the number of overlaps is to extend the two texts by means of an ontology [7], i.e., adding the words from the ontology to a text that are semantically close (hence reachable by a short path) to the words of that text. In particular, we decided to add all synonyms, hypernyms and the direct hyponyms of all words appearing in the investigated text. Hereby we follow the hypothesis of Rada et al. [16], which states that taxonomic relations are sufficient to capture semantic similarity between ontology concepts. Note that hyponyms and hypernyms may not be uniquely defined since a single word can occur in several synsets. In principle, there are two possibilities to deal with this situation:

- Use hyponyms / hypernyms of all possible synsets for the expansion
- Employ a Word Sense Disambiguation to select only the synset that corresponds to the indented meaning of the word. The drawback of this approach is that especially with short text snippets, the Word Sense Disambiguation might choose the incorrect synset, which can result in missing overlaps and therefore inexact similarity estimates.

Currently, we use possibility one but consider possibility two for a future version of our approach.

The two sets used in the Jaccard index are crisp, which means that all words are treated alike. However, the words that are newly induced by the ontology are probably less reliable for capturing the semantics of the text than the original words. Furthermore, not all of the newly introduced words are equally relevant. However, our current model cannot capture those relationships. Therefore, we extend our set representation to allow for fuzziness, i.e., we employ fuzzy sets instead of conventional crisp sets.

For conventional sets, the decision whether an element belongs to this set is always crisp, i.e., it can uniquely be decided if an element belongs to this set or not. This is different from a fuzzy set, where the membership of an element can be partial. In particular, each fuzzy set is assigned a real-valued function $\mu : X \to [0,1]$ (X: all potential elements of our set) assuming values in the interval [0,1] and specifying the degree of membership for all elements. If this membership function only assumed the values 0 or 1, the fuzzy set would actually be equivalent to a conventional set.

Set union and intersection are also defined in terms of fuzzy sets, namely in the following way:

$$\begin{aligned}\mu_{A\cap B} &= \min\{\mu_A, \mu_B\}\\ \mu_{A\cup B} &= \max\{\mu_A, \mu_B\}\end{aligned} \qquad (2)$$

The capacity of a fuzzy set is defined as the total sum over all membership values:

$$|F| = \sum_{x\in X} \mu_F(x)$$

By transferring our method to fuzzy sets, the applied similarity measure, the Jaccard index, stays unchanged. The only difference is that we compare fuzzy sets with each other and not any more conventional sets. What remains is to define the membership function. Let $Cent(A)$ be the word embeddings centroid of our original words. We then define the membership function μ as follows: $\mu(w) := (\max\{0, cos(\angle(Cent(A), Emb(w)))\})^i$ where $Emb(w)$ is the embedding vector of a word w and the use of the maximum operator prevents the membership value from being complex. The exponent i allows us to gradually adjust the influence of the word embeddings. Full influence is obtained by setting i to one. In contrast, the influence diminishes if i is set to zero.

Our similarity estimate is then used to assign user answers of several online contests to the best fitting youth milieu, which

TABLE I. EXAMPLE USER ANSWER FOR THE TRAVEL DESTINATION CONTEST (TRANSLATED INTO ENGLISH).

Choice	Country	Snippet
1	Jordan	Ride through the desert and marveling Petra during sunrise before the arrival of tourist buses
2	Cook Island	Snorkeling with whale sharks and relaxing
3	USA	Experience an awesome week at the Burning Man Festival

are *progressive postmodern youth* (people primarily interested in culture and arts), *young performers* (people striving for a high salary with a strong affinity to luxury goods), *freestyle action sportsmen*, *hedonists* (rather poorly educated people who enjoy partying and disco music) and *conservative youth* (traditional people with a strong concern for security). A sixth milieu called *special groups* comprises all those who cannot be assigned to one of the upper five milieus. For each milieu (with the exception of *special groups*) a keyword list was manually created to describe its main characteristics. For triggering marketing campaigns, an algorithm has been developed that automatically assigns each contest answer to the most likely target group: we propose the youth milieu as best match for a contest answer, for which the estimated semantic similarity between the associated keyword list and user answer is maximal. In case the highest similarity estimate falls below the 10 percent quantile for the distribution of highest estimates, the special groups milieu is selected.

The ontology we employ for our similarity estimate is Odenet, which is a freely available lexical resource recently developed by the Darmstadt University of Applied Sciences and will be explained in more detail in the next section.

III. ODENET ONTOLOGY

Freely available machine-readable lexical ontologies for German are rather sparse. On the one hand, there are websites like Wiktionary and Open-Thesaurus, which are targeted at human users. A lot of effort would have to be spent to bring the associated resources in a form that can be efficiently exploited by a computer. On the other hand, there is GermaNet [17], which is suitable both for human users as well as for automated processing. However, GermaNet is no free resource. While it may be freely used in purely academic projects, as soon as industry partners are involved, the academic license is no longer eligible and the project partners have to sign a commercial license agreement.

The lexical ontology Odenet [18][19] is devised to fill this gap. It has been automatically compiled from the Open-Thesaurus, Wiktionary, and the Open Multilingual WordNet English. Afterwards, it was manually error-checked and applied to comprehensive revisions. Similar to WordNet, semantic concepts are represented by synsets, which are interconnected by linguistic and semantic relations like hyponymy, hypernymy, meronymy, holonymy and antonymy. In total, it currently contains 120 012 lexical entries and 36 192 synsets. The entire resource is available as an XML file, which can be obtained at Github [20]. We found Odenet very easy to use and well-designed.

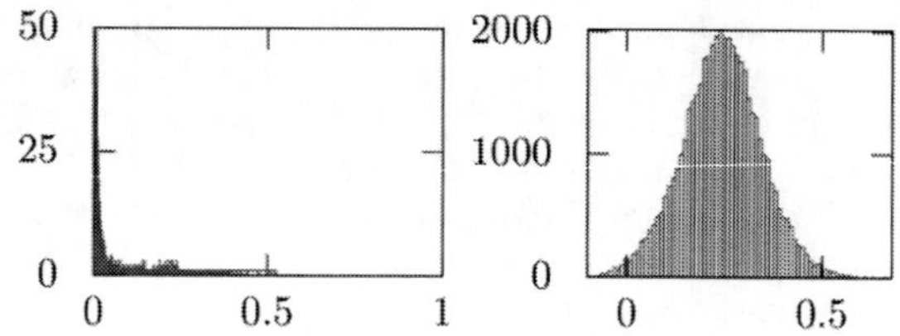

(a) Histogram for ontology-based estimate. (b) Histogram for cosine of embeddings centroids.

Figure 1. Histograms of similarity estimates.

IV. COMBINING SIMILARITY SCORES

Besides our ontology based measure, we implemented a whole bunch of other measures like ESA, cosine of word embeddings centroids, Skip-Thought vectors, etc. Usually, a stronger and more reliable similarity estimate can be obtained by combining measures. One possibility for that is majority vote, i.e., suggesting the class that most of the measures suggest. One drawback of majority vote is that the individual measures should be of comparable performance and that we need at least three of them. Furthermore, a majority vote only returns a decision for one of the classes but no (numerical) score. However, we actually need such a score to determine the 10 percent quantile (cf. previous section). An alternative to a majority vote is a weighted average. Albeit, there is again an obstacle. While all our semantic similarity estimates assume values between zero and one (Note that the cosine of word embeddings centroids can assume (usually small) negative values as well.), their distributions can be quite different (see Figure 1). Consider the case, we would like to combine cosine of word embeddings centroids and our ontology based similarity measure by a weighted sum. The first type of estimate is normally distributed and covers almost the entire value range. However, although in principle our ontology based similarity estimate can reach the value of 1, most of its values are located inside the interval [0,0.1]. To make both estimates comparable with each other, we are conducting a histogram equalization to them prior to their combination. Such an equalization levels out the relative occurrence frequencies of estimate intervals, so that the resulting values are approximately uniformly distributed. This is accomplished by transforming the similarity estimates using their cumulative probability distribution function cdf. Formally, an estimate s is mapped to the value $cdf(s)$. One downside of our method is that the resulting similarity estimate is probably biased. However, in our scenario, we are not so much interested in the actual value of our estimate but instead focus mainly on the correct ranking of target groups. Thus, the modification of the estimate's probability distribution is unproblematic.

V. EVALUATION

For evaluation, we selected three online contests (language: German), where people elaborated on their favorite travel destination (contest 1, see Table I for an example), speculated about potential experiences with a pair of fancy sneakers

TABLE II. OBTAINED ACCURACY VALUES FOR SEVERAL SIMILARITY ESTIMATES. ODENET+EMB.: LINEAR COMBINATION OF OUR ONTOLOGY BASED MEASURE WITH COSINE OF WORD EMBEDDINGS CENTROIDS. RW=RANDOM WALK BASED METHOD PROPOSED BY GOIKOETXEA ET AL. [14]

Method	Contest 1	Contest 2	Contest 3	Total
Random	0.167	0.167	0.167	0.167
ESA	0.357	0.254	**0.288**	0.335
Word2Vec Centroids	0.347	**0.328**	0.227	0.330
Skip-Thought Vectors	0.162	0.284	0.273	0.191
Odenet	0.308	0.224	0.227	0.288
Odenet+Emb.	**0.377**	0.239	0.273	**0.347**
Odenet (crisp)+Emb.	0.374	0.224	0.273	0.343
Odenet+Emb.+Mero.	0.375	0.239	0.273	0.345
RW	0.281	0.149	0.273	0.263

TABLE III. MINIMUM AND MAXIMUM AVERAGE INTER-ANNOTATOR AGREEMENTS (COHEN'S KAPPA).

Method	Contest 1	Contest 2	Contest 3
Min kappa	0.123	0.295/0.030	0.110/0.101
Max. kappa	0.178	0.345/0.149	0.114/0.209
# Annotated entries	1543	100	100

(contest 2) and explained why they emotionally prefer a certain product out of four available candidates. In bid to provide a gold standard, three professional marketers from different youth marketing companies annotated independently the best matching youth milieus for every contest answer. We determined for each annotator individually his/her average inter-annotator agreement with the others (Cohen's kappa). The minimum and maximum of these average agreement values are given in Table III. Since for contests 2 and 3, some of the annotators annotated only the first 50 entries (last 50 entries respectively), we specified min/max average kappa values for both parts.

Before automatically distributing the texts to the youth milieus, we applied on them a linguistic preprocessing consisting of tokenization, lemmatization, and compound analysis. The latter was used to determine the base form of each word, which was added as additional token. Next to our own similarity estimates, we evaluated several baseline methods, in particular ESA, cosine of word embeddings centroids, Skip-Though-Vectors, and random assignments. The accuracy values given in table Table II are obtained by comparing the automated assignment with the majority vote of the assignments conducted by our human annotators. Since the keyword lists used to describe the characteristics of the youth milieus typically consist of nouns (in the German language capitalized) and the user contest answers might contain a lot of adjectives and verbs as well, which do not match very well to nouns

TABLE IV. CORPUS SIZES MEASURED BY NUMBER OF WORDS.

Corpus	# Words
German Wikipedia	651 880 623
Frankfurter Rundschau	34 325 073
News journal *20 Minutes*	8 629 955

in the Word2Vec vector representation, we actually conduct two comparisons for the Word2Vec centroids based similarity estimate, one with the unchanged user contest answers and one by capitalizing every word beforehand. The final similarity estimate is then given as the maximum value of both individual estimates. For our proposed ontology based similarity estimate, we use the parameter settings $i := 0.5$ and weights of linear combination: 0.5, which performed best in several experiments with varying parameter values. Setting i to 0.5 seems to us as a good compromise between considering only the ontology structure ($i = 0$) and fully weighting the word embedding vectors ($i = 1$). Furthermore, we evaluated enriching the input texts with meronyms in addition to taxonomic relations, which slightly decreased the obtained accuracy (Odenet+Emb.+Mero. in Table II).

The Word2Vec word embeddings were trained on the German Wikipedia (dump originating from 20 February 2017) merged with a Frankfurter Rundschau newspaper corpus and 34 249 articles of the news journal *20 minutes*, where the latter is targeted to the Swiss market and freely available at various Swiss train stations (see Table IV for a comparison of corpus sizes). By employing articles from *20 minutes*, we want to ensure the reliability of word vectors for certain Switzerland specific expressions like *Velo* or *Glace*, which are underrepresented in the German Wikipedia and the Frankfurter Rundschau corpus.

The evaluation shows that although our ontology based method lags behind cosine of Word2Vec centroids in terms of accuracy, their linear combination performs considerably better than both of the methods alone. Furthermore, it outperforms both its crisp counterpart (exponent i:=0) and the approach of Goikoetxea et al. if applied to Odenet, used with 100 million random walk restarts, and combined with Word2Vec Word Embeddings by vector concatenation (RW in Table II). Quite striking is the poor performance of our approach on contest 2. Further analysis revealed that in several cases the correct youth milieu in this contest was indicated by only one word that was either a town name ("Basel") or a rather rare noun that are not contained in Odenet.

Note that the Odenet ontology is still under active development and contains several gaps in the semantic relations. For instance, it comprises no hyponyms of *sports*, which makes it difficult to correctly assign people to the *freestyle action sportsman* target group. Another downside is that Odenet contains no inflected forms so far. Thus we have to employ a lemmatizer in order to identify hyponyms and hypernyms for such word forms. However, the German model shipped with this lemmatizer is of rather mediocre quality. Therefore, we are currently building a suitable dataset to retrain the lemmatizer.

VI. CONCLUSION AND FUTURE WORK

We presented a similarity estimate based both on word embeddings and the Odenet ontology. In contrast to most state-of-the-art methods, it can directly employ the given ontology format. Time consuming format conversions are not necessary, which simplifies its usage significantly. The application scenario is targeted marketing, in which we aim to match people to the best fitting marketing target group based on short German text snippets. The evaluation showed that the obtained accuracy of a baseline method considerably increases if combined by a linear combination with our ontology based estimate. As future work we want to employ additional semantic relations besides hypernyms, hyponyms, synonyms and meronyms like holonyms or antonyms. Furthermore, all the model parameters are currently manually specified. It would be preferable to determine them automatically by the use of grid search or more sophisticated Artificial Intelligence methods like Bayesian search [21]. Finally, we want to experiment with other types of hierarchically ordered lexical resources, which are not necessarily ontologies, like the Wikipedia category taxonomy.

ACKNOWLEDGEMENT

Hereby we thank the Jaywalker GmbH as well as the Jaywalker Digital AG for their support regarding this publication and especially for annotating the contest data with the best-fitting youth milieus.

REFERENCES

[1] M. Lynn, "Segmenting and targeting your market: Strategies and limitations," Cornell University, Tech. Rep., 2011, online: http://scholorship.sha.cornell.edu/articles/243 [retrieved: 09/2018].

[2] H. Liu and P. Wang, "Assessing text semantic similarity using ontology," Journal of Software, vol. 9, 2014.

[3] T. Mabotuwana, M. C. Lee, and E. V. Cohen-Solal, "An ontology-based similarity measure for biomedical data - application to radiology reports," Journal of Biomedial Informatics, vol. 46, 2013.

[4] P. Resnik, "Using information content to evaluate semantic similarity in a taxonomy," in Proceedings of the 14th International Joint Conference on Artificial Intelligence (IJCAI), 1995.

[5] J. J. Lastra-Díaz and A. García-Serrano, "A novel family of IC-based similarity measures with a detailed experimental survey on WordNet," Engineering Applications of Artificial Intelligence, vol. 46, 2015, pp. 140–153.

[6] J. J. Lastra-Díaz, A. García-Serrano, M. Batet, M. Fernández, and F. Chirigati, "HESML: A scalable ontology-based semantic similarity measures library with a set of reproducably experiments and a replication dataset," Information Systems, vol. 66, 2017, pp. 97–118.

[7] M. Liu and X. Fan, "A method for Chinese short text classification considering effective feature expansion," Internation Journal of Advanced Research in Artificial Intelligence, vol. 1, no. 1, 2012.

[8] V. Oleschchuk and A. Pedersen, "Ontology based semantic similarity comparison of documents," in Proceedings of the 14th International Workshop on Database and Expert Systems Applications (DEXA), 2003.

[9] T. Mikolov, I. Sutskever, C. Ilya, G. Corrado, and J. Dean, "Distributed representations of words and phrases and their compositionality," in Proceedings of the Conference on Neural Information Processing Systems (NIPS), Lake Tahoe, Nevada, 2013, pp. 3111–3119.

[10] J. Pennington, R. Socher, and C. D. Manning, "Glove: Global vectors for word representation," in Proceedings of the Conference on Empirical Methods on Natural Language Processing (EMNLP), Doha, Katar, 2014.

[11] E. Gabrilovic and S. Markovitch, "Wikipedia-based semantic interpretation for natural language processing," Journal of Artificial Intelligence Research, vol. 34, 2009.

[12] R. Kiros et al., "Skip-thought vectors," in Proceedings of the Conference on Neural Information Processing Systems (NIPS), Montréal, Canada, 2015.

[13] M. Faruqui et al., "Retrofitting word vectors to semantic lexicons," in Proceedings of the 15th Annual Conference of the North American Chapter of the Association for Computational Linguistics (NAACL), 2015.

[14] J. Goikoetxea, E. Agirre, and A. Soroa, "Single or multiple? Combining word representations independently learned from text and WordNet," in Proceedings of the AAAI Conference on Artificial Intelligence, Phoenix, Arizona USA, 2016.

[15] C. D. Manning and H. Schütze, Foundations of Statistical Natural Language Processing. MIT Press, 1999.

[16] R. Rada, H. Mili, E. Bicknell, and M. Blettner, "Development and application of a metric on semantic nets," IEEE Transactions on Systems, Man, and Cybernetics, vol. 19, no. 1, 1989, pp. 17–30.

[17] B. Hamp and H. Feldweg, "GermaNet - a lexical-semantic net for German," in Proceedings of the ACL workshop Automatic Information Extraction and Building of Lexical Semantic Resources for NLP Applications, 1997.

[18] M. Siegel, "Talk: Odenet - a German contribution to the multilingual WordNet initiative (Odenet - ein deutscher Beitrag zur Multilingual Open WordNet Initiative)," 2017.

[19] ——, "Odenet," Linguistic Issues in Language Technology - LiLT (submitted), 2018.

[20] M. Siegel et al., "Odenet," last access: 11/12/2018. [Online]. Available: https://github.com/hdaSprachtechnologie/odenet

[21] J. Snoek, H. Larochelle, and R. P. Adams, "Practical Bayesian optimization of machine learning algorithms," in Proceedings of the Conference on Neural Information Processing Systems (NIPS), 2012, pp. 2951–2959.

International Academy, Research, and Industry Association (IARIA)
412 Derby Way
Wilmington, DE 19810

ISBN 978-1-5108-9057-2

CURRAN ASSOCIATES INC.
proceedings.com

Sixth International Conference on Smart Grids, Green Communications and IT Energy-aware Technologies (ENERGY 2016)

Held at InfoSys 2016

Lisbon, Portugal
26 - 30 June 2016

IARIA